THE CANADIAN FISHING ADVENTURE

More Enjoyment – Less Struggle…Eh?

M.C. Tatman

Dozens of suggestions, stories and hard-learned lessons.

The author gratefully appreciates **Mr. Ryan Runge** and Slate Falls Outposts, Sioux Lookout, Ontario for allowing the use of the cover image.

Mr. Runge can be reached at **SlateFallsOutposts.com**

Important Note;
In this book, the author shares experiences, methods, techniques, and products with which he and others he is familiar have found success. The author makes no guarantee the same suggestions will work in the same manner for others.

This information is provided solely for information, education, and entertainment purposes.

The author and publisher are not responsible for damages or shortcomings arising from attempts to follow these suggestions.

Copyright © 2025 by M.C. Tatman

All rights reserved. No part of this book may be used or reproduced, stored in whole or any part in any form by any means, electronic, mechanical, photocopying, recording, scanning, or otherwise, without the written permission of the author except for a reviewer who wishes to use brief quotations for a review in newspapers, magazines or other form of broadcast. For information, contact mctatman@gmail.com

ISBN # 979-8-218-50471-7
Library of Congress Control Number: 2024918518

Published by Dollar & $ense LLC®
Milford, IA 51351-7352

Table of Contents

Chapter 1
Canada Fishing, What's the Attraction? 1

Chapter 2
Selecting a Top Fishing Destination. 9

Chapter 3
Selecting Your Fishing Group 25

Chapter 4
Travel Planning 33

Chapter 5
What Do We Pack? 51

Chapter 6
First Hours in Camp. 77

Chapter 7
Finally, Out on the Lake. 83

Chapter 8
Fixing Shore Lunch. 103

Chapter 9
Heading Home. 109

Chapter 10
You'll Want to Avoid These... 117

Chapter 11
Emergencies. 123

Epilogue 127

Our Woodlands Packing Checklist 135

"It's said...the good Lord doesn't count the time we spend fishing!"

Introduction

While laughing and sharing stories with fellow fishermen and women returning from Canadian waters, others sitting with us often asked questions, curious about what it was like. You could see the wheels turning.

We had an idea: We've made a gazillion trips up north. Why not share some of our experiences with others in hopes of helping them better understand…

> What, besides great fishing, makes Canada so unique?
>
> Would it be as enjoyable for you? And–
>
> What suggestions can we pass along to help increase the fun and avoid struggles?

We imagine this book's audience as individuals who have never fished in Canada or maybe even in the US's Northwoods. We hope veteran fishermen will find ideas that might help with their next trip…and see how our experiences compare to theirs.

Our chapter, 'What Do We Pack?' is extensive. You might ask, do you bring all those things? Our answer is 'Yes,' except for a couple of optional items we point out. Each little item, in its way, has found its place in making our trips just that much better.

We encourage you to use our suggestions as a starting point and then tailor your list to suit your needs. We understand that every angler is unique and undertakes such outings with different goals.

All in our group are now retired and happily in more control of our time. When we started these trips and developed our checklists and planning, we were shoe-horning the trips into time away from work. Our goal was to make the most of those few days.

The Canadian Fishing Adventure

CHAPTER 1

Canadian Fishing, What's the Attraction?

After months of anticipation, planning, and preparation, we wake up in the dark early morning – heading to the vehicle that we packed the evening before. The air is electric with excitement. We plan to put some miles behind us before stopping for breakfast. In other northbound vehicles, we witness other groups with similar anticipation.

Our three-person group of work chums had enjoyed fishing lakes in the US Northwoods (and still do.) We had considered Canada but dismissed the thought as more expensive and too distant. That was until another group of fishermen we respected returned from a Canadian location – and were applauding the experience. The following year, we tried Canada. That was forty years ago and nearly as many outings.

This writing touches on lessons we learned visiting and fishing in Canada and the experiences we most remember.

Those fishing anywhere should find our preparation tips and hard-learned lessons of value and compare our experiences with their own.

Our planning and preparations are driven by our selfish desire

THE CANADIAN FISHING ADVENTURE

Chapter 1 – Canadian Fishing, What's the Attraction?

to have the most successful trip possible during the week we are away from work and family.

Those familiar with outdoor sports put several revered destinations on their bucket list: Wisconsin during deer season, pheasant hunting in South Dakota, and the Canadian fishing adventure.

To the author, Canada's excellent fishing is packaged in the overall experience and 'adventure' of being in another country— from the Maple Leaf flag in front of their government offices or the distance to the next town described in kilometers – or their different-looking currency (with familiar denominations), and the crisp 'eh' at the end of the locals' comments.

> *'Eh' is a brief slang term inferring agreement to a statement. But be careful; visitors will unwittingly add 'eh' to their comments after a few days.*

Don't be surprised when a motel clerk or restaurant waitress comfortably uses French to speak with the next guest.

The 'setting' is not just scenic; it's a wildlife enthusiast's dream – the vast forests have more lakes than you can count with giant rock outcroppings – revealing the Canadian *'Shield' (a hard rock strata covering the eastern half of Canada)*. And while driving the forest roads, you'll view bears, moose, foxes, eagles, etc., adding those thrills to your adventure.

US travelers in Canada will see familiar signs for brands like McDonald's, Holiday Inn Express, and Walmart. Some with the Canadian Maple Leaf added.

We also find new brands like Canadian gas stations (Petro Canada, Husky, Domo, and Irving).

The Canadian Fishing Adventure

Or Canadian banks (like RBC—Royal Bank of Canada, and CIBC—Canada Imperial Bank of Commerce), and uniquely Canadian retail businesses like Hudson's Bay, Canadian Tire, and LCBO – Ontario's liquor stores (Liquor Control Board of Ontario). The signs for Ontario Hydro are describing Ontario's electricity provider.

We find the communities of forested Canada to have a bit slower pace (another feature we welcome). They, like us, are proud of their country – you'll want to respect their pride.

When we ask fishermen what they enjoy most about their Canadian fishing trips, they mention:

Fishing lakes, where they and only a few others will visit this season.

Experiencing an afternoon where all three in the boat net dozens of 'keeper' size fish – often all three at once.

The remoteness of fishing all day and finally seeing another boat.

Come around a river bend to find a moose or bear in shallow water. Or, watch eagles grab fish near the surface – right before you. Or, a mother loon with a parade of little ones. All while enjoying the refreshing pine-scented air and the sound of water lapping the shore.

Photographing and releasing your largest trophy walleye or northern pike – and deciding which among dozens of smaller ones to keep for noon shore lunch. An everyday problem.

On each day of your trip, explore a different part of a multi-river, multi-lake, multi-bay flowage system, and find great fishing at each stop.

Chapter 1 – Canadian Fishing, What's the Attraction?

The northern woods of Minnesota, Wisconsin, and Michigan have fine fishing spots, popular with many, including this author. But if you have the time to travel further north, oh my, what tales you will share!

> *A dear neighbor and his wife spent their early married summers fishing northern Ontario lakes (both were school teachers with their summers off.) His wife still expounds on the great fishing.*

Deciding if it's for you-
Many part-time sportsmen, including this author, are excited by the thought of a few days fishing in the Canadian north woods. Let's touch on several criteria:

Age
We have seen young (<10) and older (>80) getting along well and enjoying themselves. At an Ontario boat-in camp, we witnessed a young lady from Illinois catching the largest walleye I've seen. Those with a bit of a physical handicap seem to get along just fine.

As our fishing group has gotten older, we've found it helpful to add a younger person or two to help with some of the more physical tasks (like shore lunches or portaging to out-laying lakes).

Our benchmark for young people (actually, for any guest) is their ability to contribute during chore time. Can they tie their fishing line and bait their hook? Do they pick up their gear? Are they willing helpers with basic housekeeping tasks? Every work contribution is valued in our fishing group.

> *An 82-year-old friend and I were enjoying a beverage. He had just returned from his routine early-October fishing trip to Ontario. With a beaming smile, he shares how he and his*

fishing partner caught and released 905 walleyes in five days! Way to go, Larry!

Cost

In our mind, a week of fishing 'up north' is similar to a week spent golfing or at the beach. It, of course, depends on the level of accommodation…the basic level camps we frequent are currently (2024) $1,200 – $1,500 per person for the lodge/camp fee for a 3-4 person group spending 5-6 days.

When booking reservations, expect a nonrefundable deposit of $200-$300 per person.

Lodges with optional meals will often charge less if you cook in your cabin. Additional expenses include vehicle fuel, meals, lodging to and from your fishing destination, and gear and equipment purchased in preparation. Camps charge for bait purchased (like minnows), but usually provide a set amount of outboard gas per day in the room rate.

Time devoted

We plan to spend a week away from work/home, considering about two days of traveling and four to five days of fishing. As much as I enjoy fishing, I appreciate a break after four to five days. In a bit, we'll discuss choosing your fishing group—these choices can affect the time spent together.

> *We know several retired gentlemen who, each summer, make repeated fishing trips to their favorite Canadian spot. When we leave for Ontario in mid-June, a retired neighbor was doing the same – only it was his second trip for the season (the second of 4-5 outings each season.) We miss you, Don.*
>
> *(I've often wondered, why don't they simply stay longer? We suppose they needed to check the mail.)*

Chapter 1 – Canadian Fishing, What's the Attraction?

Physical effort

You're outdoors in the elements for much of each day – with sun, rain, wind, chilled temps…and that's just day one.

One can manage the more uncomfortable elements by dressing according to conditions and adjusting one's time on the water.

When we were younger, we endured cold, rain, and wind and thought nothing of it. As we got older, we stayed in the cabin longer and enjoyed another cup of coffee rather than being the camp's first boat out for the day. And when conditions worsened, like becoming windy during an afternoon, we'd give up sooner and head back to the cabin to relax with a book.

We now tell stories about the cool mornings in a boat when we'd put our fingers in the coffee to warm them, while thinking, '*Why did I choose this?*' When, WHAM, a giant walleye hits your lure, nearly jerking the rod out of your hand. Your reel's drag sings, and you laugh and say, '*What a great day.*'

THE CANADIAN FISHING ADVENTURE

In a bit, we'll discuss the apparel you'll want to bring along to be comfortable.

So, what it boils down to, folks, if you think you can and start by looking forward to an 'up north' adventure and add some preparation (which we'll help you with), you also will have great stories to share.

CHAPTER

Selecting a Top Canadian Fishing Destination

We make our decision on Canadian fishing destinations based on two factors:

- One part is the *type of lodge/camp* we desire, and to us, of just as much importance as…
- The *structure of the lake* that lodge/camp serves.

We include this task early among 'things to do', because camp operators are busy renewing reservations with their regular guests during the winter. It was not unusual for us to have reservations made shortly after Christmas for the following June and find our preferred week filling fast. (One must imagine most fishing camps have only 5-7 cabins, and there are only a dozen weeks to their season.)

Type of accommodations.
The Canadian Northwoods fishing lodges and camps can be listed in one of three categories…

Those of which you can **drive in**, those you must **fly in**, and those you must take a **boat into**.

Drive-In

Just like its title, you can drive right to the cabin. Easy and convenient, especially for those bringing their boat. It's easier to unpack upon arrival – and repack when it's time to leave. The ease of Drive-in locations makes them a favored choice for people on their first Canadian fishing adventure.

Many drive-in camps have RV parking areas with utility hookups and access to the same camp services the cabin guests appreciate (lodge meals, boats, motors, bait, etc.).

Some Drive-In sites are the base for rental houseboats, allowing you to off-load supplies into your floating home before heading out for several days. The houseboat becomes your lodging and dining facility – and you'll fish from one of the towed fishing boats.

After a day of fishing, we enjoy hopping in the car and driving into a nearby town for ice cream, a missing grocery item, or an adult beverage. (But as I think about it, these were also the locations where the fishing was more difficult.)

Fly-In

The iconic Canadian fishing adventure is to take a float plane to an isolated lake without roads and few people. You leave your vehicle at the parking lot near the float plane dock. The staff and pilot load you and your gear and usually transport you over just 20-30 minutes (flight time) of forest to your destination camp. We found it to add $150-$250 to our trip cost (per person).

The planes and pilots themselves are noteworthy. We laugh as it's closer to riding in a freight-hauling pickup truck (part of the romance). The pilots are very skilled. They land, take off, and dock their plane a gazillion times per summer. Your destination

Chapter 2 – Selecting a Top Canadian Fishing Destination

will be just one of many stops the pilot will make that day.

We remember a young (20-ish) attractive female bush pilot. She wrestled the freight in and out of the aircraft (barrels of fuel, boxes of groceries, outboard motors, along with our gear) and then did a flawless job piloting us in and out of our camp in the brute Noorduyn Norseman. (A remarkable young lady, we hope she's still flying?)

One bush pilot had a sticker on his panel facing passengers, saying, "The size of your tip will help me remember where to pick you up." We told ourselves he was just kidding. (But, we tip pilots well, just in case.)

Once you select a 'fly-in' destination, the operators will help you with the arrangements – like where and when to meet the plane, what to bring and not bring, and what baggage weight limit they might have.

We generally flew in on Noorduyn Norseman or Beaver aircraft (look them up) or similar well-powered aircraft – we take gobs of gear and seldom reach the weight limit.

Boat In

Boat-in resorts/camps are much like fly-in camps. You and the resort staff offload your vehicle into the resort's boat, you climb on board, and they take you to the resort's dock.

One boat-in camp we've stayed at offers a fun one-hour journey through two lakes, down a river, and over a short portage. These camps often use large, high-speed launches, carrying freight, groceries, fishing gear, and excited fishermen/women.

When it's time to leave, this process is reversed.

The downside of boat-in (and fly-in) is that you're away from your car and obviously more isolated. The advantage to many is that you're more isolated, and we believe the fishing is better.

Fishermen with their boats are welcome at the boat-in camps that don't have a portage along the way.

We think arriving at your backwoods location by float plane or boat is cool.

Suggestion: Before departing your last overnight location, on the morning you are to arrive at the fishing destination, we'd suggest applying a light amount of mosquito repellent to exposed skin. Just squirt a little on your hands and wipe it on your neck, face, forehead, hands, ankles…and other exposed areas. You'll thank us when you step out of the vehicle at the float plane/boat dock or drive-in camp – one less thing to do.

Choices in Lodging

The actual fishing camp lodging usually consists of individual cabins along a lakeshore. These cabins can have very basic living conditions - or quite deluxe (with more in the 'basic' category.)

Chapter 2 – Selecting a Top Canadian Fishing Destination

At the 'basic' level, cabins can have a wood stove for heat, propane gas for cooking and grilling, and solar or generator electricity for the refrigerator/ freezer and lights. Some have hot and cold running water, indoor flush toilets, and showers. Others will have a modern bathroom facility at the end of a walk. Some still use outdoor toilets.

The fly-in and boat-in operators often have outlying **'Outpost'** cabins – a single cabin in a remote location. Outpost cabins can be basic, but surprisingly, they can also have satellite phones, Wi-Fi, and electric-start boat motors.

At most outpost cabins, the float plane stops every day or two to check on you, bring supplies, cart off trash, etc. You'll probably need your own bedding or a sleeping bag at outpost cabins.

As we have gotten older and are fortunate to have a bit more budget, we gravitate toward more comfort. Interesting, #1 in our list is an indoor bathroom (much appreciated in the middle of the night) – and even better if it includes a shower.

We also appreciate a welcoming lodge with delicious meals, Wi-Fi, comfortable boat seats, and a screened porch – perfect for an evening cocktail and cigar.

> *Yes, not only have we become spoiled, but we're also much better at justifying ourselves. We've rationalized that Wi-Fi is acceptable for a Northwoods adventure, but we insist TV and cell service is crossing the line.*

Camps we've encountered provided ample quality bedding (blankets, sheets, and pillows).

I've fought to get to sleep with crappy-thin pillows while traveling – but I didn't want to look like the old folk carrying their pillows through motel lobbies. Well, with my older age, my good sleep is more important than my ego. I now bring my favorite pillow, which is also welcome in the back seat during the vehicle trip.

You'll want to bring a few towels for bathing.

Note: In a bit, we'll include a list of questions you might ask a prospective camp operator to discover what they provide – and what you're expected to bring. We include the same questions on our checklist, just in case.

Generally, Drive-In locations will have more amenities, like full electrical service, indoor bathrooms with showers, and maybe cable TV.

A few Northwoods locations would be considered as 'deluxe' accommodations – providing more like 'Hampton Inn' type lodging, with gourmet meals, maid service, air conditioning, daily fishing guide service, satellite TV, etc. These facilities are popular with corporate groups.

Camping
We don't want to exclude those who wish to camp as an option. We know of several groups (towards the top of the 'hardy outdoorsmen' scale) who fly in with their tent and camping gear and spend several days fishing an isolated lake, camped on the shoreline, using an outfitter's positioned boat.

We have seen several tent and RV campers on the properties of Drive-In locations. They take advantage of the camp's amenities (electricity, water and sewer, fishing boats and bait, lodge dining, etc.,) while using their own set-up for lodging. We've eyed with envy those in their comfortable motor homes, with cooling air conditioners and satellite TV, while enjoying the same lakes we were fishing.

Meal expectations

We've stayed in camps where you are expected to prepare meals using your cabin's kitchen. This is fine; you just need to be prepared.

Other camps have only a refrigerator in their cabins (for cooling beverages), but no cooking is done in the cabin. They serve breakfast and the evening dinner in their lodge – and expect you to have a sandwich or shore lunch on the lake at noon.

We've never been to a camp that prepared noon lunches – except when we were blown off the lake with lousy weather. In these cases, the camp operators came to each cabin asking for the fish you'd planned for that day's shore lunch (usually filleted walleye) and shared how they planned to fix lunch for all guests. They would add a welcome bowl of hot soup and side dishes to the fried walleye…all for a welcome potluck meal.

We found lodge meals to be excellent – plentiful and tasty. Our favorite dining arrangements involve preparing breakfast in our cabin, fixing a walleye shore lunch somewhere on the lake…and dining in the lodge for the evening dinner.

Those with special dietary requirements should discuss those needs when considering a camp. With advance notice, they should be able to accommodate your requests. Remember, the food supplies arrive the same way you do – a la, over portages, by boat, by float plane, etc.

We know a fellow who was distraught whenever the food wasn't just like he had at home, silly man.

For the meals you'll be preparing, we suggest planning menus and organizing the groceries needed before leaving home. (We'll go into this later.)

A little thing we found that gives our group a respite from each other is the lodges with **open seating** for dining, where you are encouraged to sit and visit with different people. We welcomed these varied conversations after days of being with our group.

Meals are an essential part of your trip – well worth discussing with camp operators as you decide your location.

Other special needs/desires.
Every camp we've stayed in had a phone—in many cases, it was a satellite phone. Calls were a bit pricey, but you could keep in touch when that's important. I can't remember a camp where cell service worked, which we also enjoyed.

Surprisingly, many camps have internet service, which we appreciate for keeping in touch…and streaming sports and movies in the evenings.

Some camps we stayed in were within a 30-minute drive to professional medical services, while others required a float plane ride. If this is a consideration, plan accordingly. More on this later.

We had reason to visit a local community hospital in northern Canada several times. The medical attention was top-rate, and the care was professional. However, most American health insurance coverage is not valid in Canada. (They gladly welcomed MasterCard, and you can purchase health coverage for the trip.)

> *During one Northwoods hospital visit, I asked the young doctor whether he was busier in the summer or winter. He said it was usually the winter loggers who kept him most busy. I commented that most of the fishing camps probably removed their guests' fish hooks from fingers—he laughed and agreed, adding how they kindly saved the more complicated fish hook wounds for him.*

Chapter 2 – Selecting a Top Canadian Fishing Destination

Choosing a Top Lake
OK, enough on lodging and meals, let's discuss the body of water we're looking for.

From our own experiences, we have learned that the best fishing lakes have some impediments to getting to them. The easier a lake is to access – it's our experience – the more fishermen who've proceeded you – and the more challenging the fishing.

The fishing camps next to a quality road with paved boat ramps are inviting – it just makes sense that such lakes see more fishermen. Oh yes, they have fish – and may prove satisfactory. But our job in this writing is to help you tweak the best fishing trip possible for precious vacation days.

Canadian lakes are geologically relatively new. Their rocks are square – rather than the rounded stones and pebbles found in 'older' Midwest US lakes. They have fewer bait fish and less vegetation – and their fish reproduce and grow more slowly in the colder water. A walleye doesn't reach 2 lbs and 19" in length until 9-10 years old; the females aren't sexually mature until seven years old.

Understanding these challenges has made us more respectful of the resources and even more desirous of fishing water with fewer fishermen.

Over the years, we've grown fussy about the lakes we chose. Let us explain what we're looking for:

#1. Irregular shorelines
We select lakes with irregular shorelines and filled with islands - better to protect us from strong winds.

We usually only have 4-5 days to fish per trip, and while we are willing to fish in cold and rainy weather, we won't fish in dangerous waves. For that reason, we avoid large round bodies of open water – preferring a chain of narrow winding lakes with smaller bays, inlets, and points, ideally with irregularly shaped islands and winding rivers flowing in and out of similar lakes… all to allow us to remain fishing when a large open lake would have rough water conditions.

We find these irregular-shaped lakes fun to explore and believe they may hold more fish. It also gives us a chance to dust off our map-reading skills.

Of course, big round-open lakes hold fish, but when time is precious, we'd rather not lose out to high winds and waves.

#2. Avoid the masses
The Canadian lakes are made up of cold water in a rock structure with limited bait fish. (Look up the geological 'Canadian Shield'). This causes the fish to multiply and grow slowly. What makes it a super-fishing area is just one factor: most lakes have less fishing pressure!

In our experience, fishing is more challenging on lakes with numerous cottages, tourist resorts, and communities along their shore. One can assume they have more of both summer fishing pressure and ice fishermen.

The best Canadian fishing lakes (or any lakes, for that matter) are those somewhat harder to reach. For instance, if you take a short 15-20 minute floatplane flight, the cost is minimal, and you're in a far less fished body of water.

If the 'boat-in' camp you're considering has a short portage in its access journey…it's just the thing to reduce the masses – and produce excellent fishing.

It's incredible how much better the fishing is when there's an impediment between the parking lot and the fishing lake.

CHAPTER 2 – SELECTING A TOP CANADIAN FISHING DESTINATION

We view the word 'portage' as a French word for… 'hiking in the hot sun with mosquitoes.

For those wanting to use their boats, a popular TV fishing expert shares: If the boat ramp is paved and in great condition, look elsewhere; preferably, find a lake where the boat ramp is run-down – or even better, nonexistent.

#3. What fish species are you after?
We primarily fish for walleye. We love catching and eating them and taking a few home. Sure, we enjoy fighting a northern pike, bass, or even a muskie - but our first choice is walleye.

There's no science to this, but we've observed that fishing camps and lodges rank their more prominent fish species in order in their advertising. When they advertise, *'Northern pike, bass, perch, and walleye'* it's unlikely a top walleye lake.

Whatever fish species you're after, you might find more success at a lake where the fish camp lists that species first. *'Walleye, northern pike and lake trout.'*

The Canadian Fishing Adventure

Resources for finding fishing lakes

For northwest Ontario (north of Minnesota), the '*NW Ontario (Sunset Country) Lodging Guide* ' is especially good, as it breaks out the different types of lodging…fly-in camps, drive-ins, boat-ins, houseboat providers, and campsites.

You can see if the fishing camp you're considering has a road leading to it, whether there are other camps on the same body of water, and a rough idea of the size and shape of the body of water and its connecting waters.

The Sunset Country Travel Guide and Fishing Map is available free on their informative website:
https://visitsunsetcountry.com/places-to-stay

For other Canadian provinces, these resources might give you some ideas:

Quebec

https://www.pourvoiries.com/en/activities-and-services/fishing

Manitoba

https://huntfishmanitoba.ca/

https://www.gov.mb.ca/nrnd/fish-wildlife/pubs/fish_wildlife/fish/angling-guide.pdf

https://huntfishmanitoba.ca/blog/

Saskatchewan

https://www.tourismsaskatchewan.com/things-to-do/fishing/fishing-and-hunting-guide

https://saskborder.com/fishing

https://www.todocanada.ca/15-great-places-fish-saskatchewan/

Alberta

https://www.travelalberta.com/things-to-do/outdoor-activities/fishing

https://fishingbooker.com/blog/alberta-fishing/

British Columbia

https://www.gofishbc.com/

https://britishcolumbia.com/things-to-do-and-see/bc-fishing-and-guides/

https://www.sunshinecoastcanada.com/

Northwest Territories

https://spectacularnwt.com/activities/fishing/

https://fishlodges.com/northwest-territories-canada-fishing-lodges/

THE CANADIAN FISHING ADVENTURE

We have attended Outdoor & Travel Expos for fishing destination ideas. We enjoy visiting with the camp operators and asking them questions (like those we share below). Some of the Expos are devoted to Canadian locations.

Of course, they'll tout their excellent fishing. But by using the tips we've shared on selecting a fishing lake, along with your accommodation/meal desires, you can choose a winner. Remember:

– Avoid large open bodies of water; seek irregular shorelines with multiple bays, islands, and, ideally, rivers connecting to other similar lakes.

– Some separation from the masses.

– And in their own words (advertising), is their featured fish species what you're after?

Chapter 2 – Selecting a Top Canadian Fishing Destination

Word of mouth

We've had good luck and bad following friends' recommendations on choice Canadian fishing sites. Looking back, the problem sites all violated one or more of our three rules – and reinforced in our minds the importance of our criteria.

We had a dear friend who went on about his group's favorite fishing lake. On and on. We always enjoyed trying new spots, so we made reservations, anxious to try it. There was a small town on the lake's shore, with numerous summer homes and a full-blown tourist resort. Lordy.

We're pretty good at finding walleye…but at this lake, we struggled. The fishing was terrible. We did enjoy buying bait from the cute girls staffing the bait dock…which, as we think back – was the location's only high point.

When we again met with our friend, we shared our struggles and poor success. Ha, and he said, 'Ya, the last year or two, we've had a harder time there ourselves.'

Questions we ask lodge representatives when considering their location: (Assign your priorities, these are ours…)

Lodging:
- Are toilet and shower facilities in the cabin?
- Does the cabin have running hot & cold water? Ice?
- What is the cabin's heat source?
- Is electricity available? Internet? Phone?
- Number of people per sleeping room?
- Is bedding provided? Towels?

Meals:
- Have them explain their meal options.
- Is cooking allowed in the cabin?

- Can they prepare a 'shore lunch' box? LP burner?
- Does the lodge sell groceries? Beer/Liquor?

Fishing:
- What size and type of fish are being caught daily?
- Have them describe their boats, motors, and baits available.
- Do they provide dip nets, minnow buckets, and boat seats with backs?
- Do they have 'fishing guide' services?
- What are the lake's fish 'in possession' limits?
- Is there a fish cleaning shack? A fish freezer?

Miscellaneous:
- How do they prefer to be paid? Cashier's check? Credit card? Cash?
- Do they sell fishing licenses?
- Nearest medical service. Ask them to describe what to expect if a health emergency arises.

CHAPTER

Selecting Your Fishing Group

I'm sure our fishing group was formed like most – several work chums who arrived at the idea over an after-hours cocktail. You've known each individual for some time and enjoy each other's company – what could go wrong, eh?

Let's share some suggestions to ward off problems. You're going to be 'together' for a number of hours - in the vehicle, in the cabin, and in the boat.

Several issues you'll want to address early:

A past DWI conviction
Canada views 'driving while under the influence' of alcohol or drugs (DWI) as a felony – much more seriously than the US does.

Canadian Border officials have access to US criminal record information. As we understand, they don't check everyone. Still, if they do and discover a person in your group having a past DWI, that person will likely be refused entry, whether entering as a passenger or pedestrian, even if they have no intent to drive in Canada.

We've heard of groups where this occurred. The others in the group had to make the uncomfortable decision of leaving their buddy. And their buddy was forced to call someone at home to drive to the border to get him/her. Lovely.

Ontario does provide a waiver for those who prepare in advance. A person seeking an entry waiver can contact Canada's Border Services Agency at 506-636-5064 or 204-983-3500 or visit http://cbsa-asfc.gc.ca/noncan-eng.html.
(We cannot imagine a worse bureaucratic hassle.)

On Google, several service providers (law firms) offer assistance in these situations, which sounds like a better approach.

Those organizing the trip – will want to ask potential participants early on if they've had a past DWI. Those seeking a waiver will want to start the process early.

Getting a passport
Everyone will need a passport to enter Canada and to re-enter the USA.

If you don't have a passport – or if yours needs renewing – this will take about two months, so you'll want to work on this early.

We discuss this more in the 'Travel Planning' section.

Now let's consider the individuals you have in mind:

Individuals with a difficult personality
You may accommodate the opinionated co-worker while having lunch at the company lunchroom. If they have to win discussions, have their way with choices, discredit the thoughts of others, or find it essential to correct others, try to visualize a week closely together.

Chapter 3 – Selecting Your Fishing Group

This person differs from a leader who decides and turns to the group, asking for their concurrence.

While interviewing prospective workers, we have a dear friend who would ask himself, *'Could I stand spending a day in a fishing boat with this person?'* My friend found this a valuable hiring test.

Individuals with excessive behaviors should give you cause for thought, like…talking too much, being too negative, drinking or smoking too much, or strongly sharing political views. A week of such behavior will get old.

You won't change such behavior – it is well-rooted. You have two options: Try to ignore the troublesome behavior, or avoid inviting that person.

Persons who don't fit
People enjoy spending time with people who are similar to them, those with similar values, interests, experiences, beliefs, etc. Visiting and being together is comfortable.

A person with a different 'chemistry' may be a fine person, and accommodating these differences may be worthwhile as we work to get along and get to know the person. However, such accommodations can be tiresome over an extended period, turning a fun outing into a sour experience.

Some differences in people add interest and variety – it's the character we enjoy in the person. When these 'differences' are overpowering, you have two choices: agree to accept or ignore the issue – or not invite the person.

To this category, we add those individuals who've demonstrated their unwillingness to lift their weight in duties. There will be housekeeping, boat keeping, meal preparation, etc. Anyone not willing to do their part requires others to do more. Whether it's a young person or an older person, we doubt if anyone is signing on as a group member to clean up after someone else.

Those who can't afford the trip
I'm sorry, but we all have different financial statuses; that's how it is. Some can afford the type of outing we're describing – unfortunately, some cannot.

We'll try to describe the costs and preparations involved, so people can decide if this factor will be a problem.

Another behavior issue of concern is the penny-pincher. This person can afford the trip but is so 'tight' that they present constant pushback over expenses (like fuel costs, on-route lodging, meals while traveling, buying bait, etc.). You would have witnessed this in the individual while back home – a week together won't improve it.

Is it a place for women and young people?
Yes, of course, it would make a great family adventure. If the woman is comfortable outdoors and enjoys fishing, she'll do fine. We get a kick when women in a group out-fish the fellows.

As we've shared, we suggest that when a young person can take care of their needs, help with general tasks, rig up and bait their hook, and remove their fish – Voilá, bring them along!

How many individuals should we include?

We've gone with groups of 3, 4, 5, and 6 individuals. Each number presents its planning issues. We've been in camps where individuals were staying by themselves. And many occasions of

Chapter 3 – Selecting Your Fishing Group

just two fellows, husband-wife couples, and grandfathers with grandsons.

The camps have cabins built to accommodate groups of various sizes. We've found 2 or 3 to be a good number in a vehicle, even for vehicles able to hold more. (Who wants to be 'packed in' for hours?)

We found it best to use a second vehicle, which we grew to appreciate for numbers above three individuals. This allowed passengers room to stretch out and accommodate differing travel arrangements.

Two people in a 14-16' boat works well. Three individuals are the most camps usually allow in a 16' boat – and the most we've found to work well. The person in the back operates the motor and depth finder, and the person in the middle seat is busy helping with the dip net, putting fish on the stringer, passing bait from the minnow containers, etc. Usually, the person in front watches out for rocks and sleeps.

You'll need a second boat for groups larger than three individuals. With more than one boat, we appreciate low-priced Motorola two-way radios for boat-to-boat chatter (either family radio service – FRS band, or their bit stronger GMRS units). Two-way radios are handy for bragging about a giant fish just caught or where to meet for shore lunch.

For variety, we enjoy changing fishing partners in the boats each day.

Suggestions:
We're thankful our group gets along quite well. Still, a week of nearly constant togetherness draws on us. Some things we do to prevent wearing on each other:

Each person is assigned a responsibility. Someone needs to be the group leader – the spokesperson with the lodge operators. Someone needs to be the cook. Someone needs to prepare the boat(s) – fuel, bait, etc., in the mornings. Others not in these duties can help with fish cleaning, dishwashing, getting ice, and tidying up the cabin.

It would be helpful if one or two of your group members were experienced in boat handling and operating an outboard motor. It's best if one or two have map-reading skills. It would also be valuable to have someone familiar with fish cleaning. (In the weeks leading up to our trips, we brush up on some of these skills by watching YouTube – along with videos on fishing techniques.)

We found it worked well for us each to put $50 or $100 in a kitty and have a designated person responsible for those monies – to pay for the group's lesser purchases along the way, like groceries, bridge tolls, meals, etc. We found it easier and more fair than individuals taking turns paying. We'd laugh as our group monies were kept in a velvet Crown Royal whiskey bag. We applied leftover funds to the next trip's groceries.

In the car for hours, we enjoy using the back seat as an escape, where we can wear headphones and listen to an audiobook, or read a book, or nap. For several hours, you're in your world. Tell the others it's nothing personal; you just want to read/listen to your book or nap. Those in the vehicle's front seat can continue visiting - keeping the driver alert.

In the evening, some journey off to their bed, listening to headphones, reading a book, or doing something on their laptop. Some find solace sitting on the porch with a cigar.

We'd take along popular movies and TV series for the group to watch in the evening. We've found ourselves especially enjoying

Chapter 3 – Selecting Your Fishing Group

old Boston Legal episodes viewed on a laptop.

As mentioned earlier, we welcomed lodge dining rooms that encouraged open seating. We get to spend time with new people.

Some in our group would take walks after dinner, exploring the camp and its surroundings. Each would bring back their stories of discovery. In the evenings, some of our group and other guests often would venture down to the camp's boat docks with an adult beverage.

> *...one like that?*
> *After dinner at one camp, we wandered about ¼ mile down a trail through the woods to where they placed trash. We wondered if we'd see a bear or two. And sure enough, after a few moments, a couple of small bears would come into the clearing. We'd watch them from a distance and quietly leave.*
>
> *As we returned to the camp facilities, the camp operator asked where we had been. We told him we'd been to the dump area looking for bears. He said, "You mean one like that?" Pointing to a small bear in between our cabin and another.*

We learned our relations were better when we were better rested, avoided drinking too much, and pulled back from "conflict activities" like discussing politics or playing serious poker. (More on this when we discuss things best avoided.)

> *A dear friend shared after his group had just returned from Canada, "We'll be better friends again in 4-5 weeks."*

The best friends – even married couples, need their own space for a period. There's nothing wrong with that. Giving it a little thought in advance will allow you to arrange your quiet periods.

The Canadian Fishing Adventure

Her limit in minutes
One evening in a fly-in camp, we noticed the lodge's cook had finished her kitchen duties and was on her way to the boat dock with a can of beer and a fishing rod.

As we watched from our porch, she caught several nice walleyes in just minutes – lordy. We had good fishing that day, but we'd boated over miles of lakes and rivers.

Several in our group grabbed a beer and fishing rod and went to join her. Returning later, they reported that her fishing success was a nightly occurrence. Maybe it was the beer?

CHAPTER 4

Travel Planning

Once you've chosen who's going with you, there are a couple of tasks each needs to consider – the first several are of special concern because you're dealing with government bureaucracies. For that reason, you'll want to start working on them early.

Passports
Each traveler planning to enter Ontario will need a current passport. (Those with an existing passport should check to ensure it hasn't expired – for adults, passports usually expire after ten years, which is such a long period that one forgets about them.)

Passports cost $130 and last for 10 years (for adults); at the time of this writing (2024), the issuance and renewal wait times are 2-3 months. (Expedited applications take 1-2 months.)

The steps needed to apply for a passport can be found here:
https://www.us-passport-service-guide.com/obtain-a-us-passport.html

This young lady describes how to renew your passport:
https://www.youtube.com/watch?v=6soDC0AsspM

Non-residents Fishing in Ontario
Ontario requires <u>two</u> cards to fish legally.

First, Ontario requires those 18 and older to obtain an Ontario Outdoors Card, a plastic identification card, currently costing

$8.57 (Canadian$). It can be purchased online at: https://www.ontario.ca/page/get-outdoors-card-and-licence-summary

or visit: huntandfishontario.com. Or call: 1-800-387-7011.

The Ontario Outdoors Card is good for three years (starting the year it's issued); it can be renewed using the same contacts listed above.

It's currently reported that once you apply, it can take 20-30 days to obtain the Outdoors Card by mail. To be safe, we'd suggest each member of your group apply early.

Those under 18 do not need an Ontario Outdoors Card or a fishing license if they're with a licensed adult. However, their catch is part of that adult's limit. Youth are welcome to have their own Outdoors Card and license and then be able to possess their own limit.

You must have the Ontario Outdoors Card to obtain a fishing license (or, as Canadians spell it, *licence*). However, you can get both with the above online source or phone number.

The second card needed to fish in Ontario is the fishing license; they offer two options:

A Sport Fishing license allows the full limit for the lakes and species fished; an 8-day non-resident license costs $54.35

(Canadian$) and $83.19 for a full year. (2024 pricing)

Or a Conservation Fishing license calls for a reduced limit. An 8-day non-resident license costs $31.52 (Canadian$) or $52.17 for a full year.

Ontario offers a convenient 1-day license for $24.86 (Canadian$); the Outdoors Card is unnecessary.

At this writing, Ontario's Ministry of Natural Resources and Forestry has divided Ontario into several management areas. The area where we usually fish allows four walleye and four northern pike in possession under the Sport license. And two walleye and two northern pike in possession with the Conservation license.

In past years, our group has taken advantage of the Conservation license (included in our lodging fee at camps we frequent). We catch and release fish all day, keep a couple for shore lunch, and, if we desire, freeze two (per species, per person) to take home.

If you're going to an Ontario fishing destination that provides complimentary Conservation licenses, and you're OK with the reduced daily limit, we'd recommend you get your license in that manner. If not, we'd suggest getting the Outdoors card and license from Ontario's website:

https://www.ontario.ca/page/fishing-licence-non-residents-canada

Individuals in the group can choose different licenses.

Each of Canada's provinces has its own fishing and licensing regulations (much like US states). Several provinces require an identification card (like the Ontario Outdoors Card). You can obtain a non-resident license in various ways: (i.e., via an online site, phone, in person at authorized retail locations, and from authorized fishing camp operators).

US citizens with DWI convictions

In our 'Selecting your Fishing Group' section, we discuss Canada's treatment of those attempting to enter who have a past DWI conviction. You'll want to refer to that if this affects someone in your group.

When is it best to go?

Many feel that June is the best month for fishing Canada's popular species...walleye, northern pike, bass, and lake trout – followed by fall.

Like the US, the legal fishing seasons differ per Canadian province, often by zone or particular lake, and species.

By the end of May, most fishing seasons for the different species are open. The camp(s) you're considering will share the dates their camp will open, which usually mirrors the fish opening and ice going out.

We fished the first week of June and found ourselves among the first at that camp for the season. We had a touch of snow flurries as we arrived, followed by 70-degree days.

A dear friend, who has fished Canadian lakes since a young boy, says the very best fishing when a person can make it...is 14 days after the ice goes out. Which speaks well for a late May or early June trip.

Our friends who make 4 to 5 trips each season make a trip or two in June – followed by several more summer and fall trips. They adjust their fishing techniques as the weather warms – as most fish move deeper. It's usually easier to make reservations past June – and the fish re still there.

I've spoken of a friend whose one annual trip to Canada is in early October. Their group loves the fishing excitement with the Fall colors.

Planning the travel time

The Fly-in camps will arrange the float plane for you and share instructions on the time and location to meet your float plane. You and the pilot will transfer your gear from your vehicle to the aircraft, weighing it in the process.

The Fly-In and Boat-In camps often ask us to arrive mid-morning on our first day. They ask us to call them from the last town on our journey (30 – 60 minutes out) so they can schedule a time to meet us.

Arriving in camp mid- or later morning fits our plans. It allows us time to move in our gear and get settled, arrange the boat(s) and bait, take along some lunch, and head out for a part-day of fishing.

We live about 13 hours from our most frequented Canadian fishing locations. We drive about 11 hours and stay overnight in a Canadian motel. The next day, we shop for last-minute grocery items and finish the remaining distance to our destination - allowing us to easily arrive mid-morning.

Caution: If your travel plans include spending a night in a motel en route, we suggest making reservations long in advance. Accommodations are limited in these smaller communities – as other fishermen and regular travelers have the same thoughts.

We'll visit later about the items we pack, but let us insert here – at the last town we pass through on the route to our fishing location, we purchase our perishable groceries (eggs, milk, bread, etc.).

Crossing the Border
Border officials' rules and requests can change quickly. We'd suggest checking online or visiting with someone who recently made the crossing to see what the officials are requesting.

At the time of this writing, entering Canada and re-entering the U.S. is what we'd call 'normal.' There are no special medical requests or hoops to jump through - like during the days of the COVID-19 virus.

Everyone entering, whether by car or aircraft, commercial or private (general aviation), will need a valid passport.

We understand youth under 16 need to prove U.S. citizenship (why not get a passport?).

Children traveling with only one parent must have a notarized statement of approval from the absent parent, allowing the travel and including the trip dates.

Border no – no's
Firearms and mace are not allowed. (There are hoops to jump through to gain an exception, but we think it's easier just to leave

the guns and mace at home.)

Under the rules at the time of this writing, some fresh fruits, vegetables, and non-packaged food items are allowed. Lordy. If you decide to go this route and you say, *"We have a week's worth of fresh fruit and vegetables."* We can picture officials ordering you to unpack all for review.

Do yourself a favor. Use the Canadian grocery stores – we've found them as modern and well-stocked as any in the States. Less chance for delay.

What to expect at the Border
You'll likely be in a line of vehicles. This is a good time to ensure you have your passport in hand, remove your sunglasses, and roll down the front and back driver's side windows.

As you near the border patrol window, signs will instruct you to hold your vehicle back somewhat until you're signaled to proceed. (At this point, both the Canadian and when you return…the U.S. Border authorities will be videotaping you and your vehicle from multiple angles, running your car's license plate number, and who knows what else.)

When it's your turn to move your vehicle ahead to the window, all occupants need to look the official in the eye and answer questions in an earnest, straightforward manner.

Questions to expect from the Canadian Border officials (and ideal answers)

Where do you live? (to all occupants, answer: town & state)

You are citizens of what country? (answer from each, USA)

What is the purpose of your visit? (answer, fishing)

Where are you going? (answer, name of fishing camp)

What are you bringing in? (answer-clothing and fishing gear)

Are you bringing anything to leave (gifts, etc.)? (answer – no)

Are you bringing in any firearms, tobacco, or alcohol? (we declare the duty-free liquor we just purchased; it's usually still sitting in the passenger area).

We have the driver answer all questions unless the official asks others to answer.

Every border crossing official we've encountered is serious. They have complete authority over whether you enter or not (without explaining their decision). Your answers, and more importantly, your mannerisms and behavior, must be attentive and serious. This especially applies to young males (< 25 years old).

During crossings, we've often witnessed a vehicle ordered to pull over, unload, and open all baggage and gear onto the parking lot surface (yes, quite the mess). In these situations, the occupants usually included one or two young men.

We enjoy taking our young male family members fishing and encourage you to do the same. It's important to realize that in front of the border patrol officer is not the place for joking around – if you're seeking a no-hassle entry.

When making a mid-afternoon Friday or Saturday border entry into Ontario, we've experienced l-o-n-g lines (1 hour+). We'd suggest crossing earlier in the day. It's usually mid-morning when we reach the US border for re-entry; the wait is just minutes.

Chapter 4 – Travel Planning

Duty-free purchases
The USA and Canada border towns often have duty-free stores for travelers exiting their countries. The products' normal taxes don't apply, as they won't be consumed in that country.

We like to stop at the duty-free store to purchase low–priced, top–shelf liquors. You can take 1.14 liters (40 oz) of liquor into Canada and 1.14 liters when re-entering the US.

Some of us will hop out of our vehicle while in the waiting line - leaving the driver to move the vehicle along, while the rest of us run into the duty-free store and make our purchases (including one for the driver).

You choose the liquor you want in the store, pay for it, and get a receipt. Each store has a method of transferring the actual bottle to you as your vehicle is committed to crossing. If asked, you'll want to report this 1.14-liter of alcohol to the upcoming border official.

Remember, as you enter Canada, you will stop at the Canadian border station. You won't stop at the US border station until you're ready to leave Canada and re-enter the US.

Preparing your vehicle, boat, and trailer for the trip
Before venturing on any lengthy trip, we like to have our vehicle, boat, and trailer looked over by professionals. Again, you've waited for months for this week, and the others in your group have expectations. No one wants to be stranded on an isolated forest road – awaiting help.

Take your vehicle to a quality shop and have it serviced (lube, filters, wipers, etc.). Have them check the tires, the brakes, coolant, lights – everything, including the spare tire and the jack and lug wrench used for changing tires. I've even told mechanics, *'I'll be traveling in the Northwoods – miles from repair shops – so do a good job.'*

Then, before the trip, wash the vehicle thoroughly inside and out, including the windows. No one wants to travel for hours in a dirty vehicle.

Every trip into and out of the forest, we pass a small boat or utility trailer broken down with tire or axle problems. If you pull a trailer, have a quality tire dealer check the tires for age and travel speed, lube the bearings, and examine brakes, springs, and axles for issues.

Small trailer tires turn many times more than larger car or pickup tires…causing hotter temperatures and more wear. Pack a spare wheel and tire for the trailer.

We own a boat and view it as the world's least dependable mode of transportation. Before the trip, we suggest taking your boat to the dealer and thoroughly checking it – especially the battery, fuel system, and parts that need lubrication.

When operating our own boat in strange waters – miles from a service shop – we have at least one spare propeller tucked away, along with the tools needed to change it. We carry battery jump packs, one in the vehicle, and another in the boat. We also carry duct tape for the many things it can mend, like a hole poked in the hull.

Yes, even with all the precautions, we may still have a breakdown, but it's not because we didn't prepare.

We appreciate these trips prompting us to conduct thorough maintenance reviews. It leaves us more confident during the trip and for months afterward.

CHAPTER 4 – TRAVEL PLANNING

Without being too personally intrusive, it also helps our enjoyment during outings to have matters at home and work dealt with and in good order. It helps us better relax to not have worrisome issues in the background.

Purchases in Canada
Today (2024), a gas pump in a Northwoods community indicates the fuel price is $159.9. (Some Canadian gas stations share the cost in 'cents' – a holdover from when prices were lower; others show the price with the decimal two positions left, which we in the US are familiar with, like $1.599.)

The price is per metric liter, in Canadian dollars – let's convert it to what we're more familiar with. A liter is close to the same volume as a quart, and four liters is close to a gallon. So, $1.599 x four = $6.396 for approximately a gallon of fuel in Canadian dollars.

The value of US and Canadian funds changes constantly. This week in 2024, the US $1 is worth $1.36 Canadian (it can be the reverse). Just enter the dollar amount in Google asking for that day's conversion from Canadian to US (or vice versa), and viola, the $6.396 per gallon Canadian is $4.73 in US funds.

That's a better price, but still higher than we're used to. Canada, nationally and in most of its provinces, charges sizable sales taxes to fund things like health coverage.

These sizable sales taxes also apply to the lodging and fishing camp fees. (There was a reimbursement provision for those visiting Canada to reclaim a portion of the lodging tax. This provision has been discontinued. They didn't take away much; it required a blizzard of receipts and paperwork and, at best, yielded only a portion of the lodging taxes.)

We have tried various strategies for paying for Canadian purchases, including having some monies converted at Canadian banks. This usually left us with Canadian currency to carry over to the following year's purchases.

We find our credit cards work best for purchases. That day's conversion rate is automatically applied with no fee or hassle. The car owner's credit card pays for fuel, the amount is converted to US funds using Google, and the driver is reimbursed by the group.

Canadian currency shares the same denominations as US currency-dollars, quarters, dimes, etc. But you will find they have a distinct appearance. (Interestingly, while they are still in circulation, Canada's mint no longer produces pennies.)

Two coins are iconic – the Canadian one-dollar coin is nicknamed the 'Loonie' for its loon (water bird) symbol, and its sister, the two-dollar coin, is called the 'Toonie.'

Canada's $2 Toonie & $1 Loonie coins

CHAPTER 4 – TRAVEL PLANNING

$1 paper note

You'll find Canada is more metric-based than the US. Here are some handy ways to convert metric measurements to America's English system:

A metric **kilometer (km)** equals .62 miles. For a quick conversion, a person can approximate two kilometers being slightly more than a mile.

An easy, but closer conversion is to divide the kilometer amount by two, divide that answer by 4, and then add the two numbers together.

200km / 2 = 100. Then 100 / 4 = 25, and 100 + 25 = 125 miles. It's not exact, but it's close.

A speed limit of 60 km per hour divided by 2= 30. Then 30 / 4 = approximately 7…adding 30 + 7 equals approximately 37 mph. Again, not exact, but close enough to avoid a speeding citation.

The speedometers on many cars make for a straightforward conversion, showing miles per hour next to kilometers per hour.

The Canadian temperature is measured in degrees **Celsius (C)** (with water freezing at zero and boiling at 100). It's more condensed than the Fahrenheit (F) scale.

To quickly convert in your head, take the Celsius temperature times two, and add 30. So, 10 degrees C times two equals 20 + 30 = 50 degrees Fahrenheit. It's not exact, but within a couple of degrees, you'll know if you'll need a coat.

Packing your gear for travel
After several occasions of unloading or reloading gear in pouring rain, we prefer hard poly totes with wheels if we're heading to a boat-in camp. All clothing, personal items, soft tackle bags, reels, depth finders, packaged grocery items, small fans, etc., go into the tote(s).

Last-minute grocery items (milk, eggs, bread, ground beef, etc.) are packed at the grocery store in cardboard boxes. We have sturdy trash bags ready to protect these boxes from rain. The same applies to a cardboard box for our liquor, soda, and beer.

For Fly-In locations, we'd stay with soft-sided (duffle) baggage - the pilots appreciate smaller, easier-to-pack items. (Besides, they're not likely to be traveling in heavy rain.)

Rods travel in a sturdy carrying tube. We use two-piece rods, especially for fly-ins. We loosely tie the top and bottom rod shafts together with ties – and place several rods in a tube. We then add a towel to the tube to prevent excessive vibration.

One or two in our group take a laptop (even in the far Northwoods, most camps have wi-fi), allowing us to catch the news, play games, watch movies, etc. We put the laptop in a large zip-lock bag, then inside its travel bag – and that goes in another plastic bag. I then hold the laptop during the boat-in or fly-in trip. (You won't look unusual.)

Caution: For Boat-In and Fly-In locations, another group and their gear may travel with you in the plane or boat. If so, the gear will be co-mingled. So, before leaving home, clearly label your gear – and count the number of your items. At each transfer point, re-count that your items are still with you.

Believe us, the gear can quickly get mixed.

We were unloading the float plane after a fun week of fishing when, somehow, my tackle box went home with another group. People were anxious to be on their way – and a mistake was made. When discovered, the other folks were as concerned as I was – and before long, my tackle box was back where it belonged. We now do a better job labeling and counting our gear.

That's Ned!
After a long day of driving, we were glad to finally pull into the Dryden, Ontario motel, where we had reserved rooms. Our fishing destination was another two hours away, and we were expected to arrive the following morning.

After the long drive, the three of us entered one of our motel rooms to have an adult drink. The group's senior turned and said, "There's something I need to share with you guys."

Lordy, we thought, what could this be, we've been together in the car for hours, and it couldn't have been mentioned then.

Our senior says, "Two weeks ago, a fellow in my hometown named Ned died. Ned wanted his ashes to be sprinkled on a certain island in Canada."

We looked at each other and said, "So." Our senior responded, "Well, that bag in the back seat propping up your pillow - well, that's Ned!" (his ashes)

We were surprised and then said, "Why wait until now to tell us?" To which he responded, "I didn't want you guys to act suspicious going through the border."

To which we said," Oh my yes, that question comes up often. Do you have any alcohol? Any tobacco? Any – body remains?"

The following day, we delivered Ned's ashes to the fishing camp along our route. The camp operator was happy to receive them and shared that they had a ceremony planned – and it wasn't their first for that season. We learned that Ned was not a fisherman; instead, he hunted moose.

A noticeable 'list'

After a day of fishing, our group often gathered at a lodge bar to visit and have a beverage. Before long, one of us would laugh and bring up a similar night, years before.

A night when we had entered a restaurant and felt a noticeable 'list' to the floor when we walked in. But we each had said nothing. We all laughed when our drinks came and we saw how the liquid was not level in the glasses. We'd each held back saying anything when we first walked in, thinking our own wiring was amiss.

The building had a charming slant – the owners should have marketed it.

Sand volleyball

In one of the en-route Canadian communities we were staying in overnight, we came upon a charming little restaurant. On this evening, the dining room and bar area were full, but there was room in the back overlooking a sand volleyball court, where we enjoyed the local young people playing a heated game. We got caught up, and soon, we were also cheering – mainly for the girls' teams.

In future trips, as we entered the same restaurant and were asked if we'd like a seat in the dining room – we'd say, 'Oh no, we'd prefer to overlook the volleyball court.'

Embarrassing moment
A dear friend recently took his two grandsons to Canada fishing. At the border entry, the official asked him to lower the rear window. Suddenly worried, our friend (in a new-unfamiliar vehicle) said he didn't think that window would lower (thinking of the tailgate window). Thankfully, his grandson piped up, saying, 'Grandpa, I think she wants the rear passenger window lowered.'

Our friend quickly tries to lower that window – which, of course, doesn't work. His grandson again tried to help, saying, 'I think the child lock is on'. Our friend looks at the border guard and says, 'I don't know how to open it.' To which the border official sharply stated, 'Are you sure this is your vehicle?'

Friend Matt says they were permitted entry and had a super trip.

CHAPTER

What Do We Pack?

When traveling to a remote location, it's important to remember essential items along with a few 'nice-to-have' items.

I divide my packing into the <u>travel</u> portion of the outing, the <u>fish</u>ing items, and the <u>cook</u>ing items. We'll explain which items go where and what makes certain items essential. Then, we share our full **Packing Checklist** on page 135 which should help you develop your own.

For traveling to and from

I pack the 'travel' items in a smaller duffle bag, which is handy for taking into motels...and serves as a place for important items – that are easier to access versus digging through all the fishing gear.

- Billfold (driver's license, credit cards, and cash – I take $200)
- Cell phone & charger (you'll likely have no cell service in camp, but it's also a camera and GPS device)
- Passport
- Sunglasses
- Map/directions to the destination & their phone number

- Payment for fishing camp (blank check, cashier's check, whatever)

- Health insurance card

- Auto insurance card and registration (in the vehicle glovebox)

- Flashlight – with its fresh batteries

- Spare eyeglasses

- Spare car keys

I welcome these items for use while traveling and in the cabin:

- Good paperback, 1-2 magazines

- Digital device, headphones & charger (for listening to music, audiobooks…)

A dear friend would say…'You can tell a lot about a person by the 'grip' they carry.' We miss you, Everett!

Packing for the fishing camp

If you're heading to a Fly-in camp, you'll want to pack these items in larger soft-sided duffle bags. They fit better in aircraft.

For Boat-In camps, we use watertight cargo totes. These poly containers need wheels on one end, lids that latch down tightly and won't blow off, and a sturdy handle.

Chapter 5 – What Do We Pack?

We point out again: Boldly label each of your luggage items – and count the number.

Those going to Drive-in camps can pack their gear however they want.

While traveling, I'll either wear a pair of slacks or cargo shorts, depending on the weather. Whichever pair I wear, the other is packed. (These are kept clean for evenings in the lodge and for the return trip home.)

- A pair of underwear and a polo shirt for each travel day
- A pair of socks for each travel day
- One sweater or sweatshirt
- One handkerchief packed, plus one in the slacks you're wearing
- Comfortable shoes for travel and the lodge

I take two pairs of shoes for the trip, one comfortable pair like tennis or boat shoes for traveling and evenings in camp and lodge…and a second pair of outdoor footwear worn in the boat, packed in the cargo tote.

- Toiletries kit…traveling in the small duffle

- Toothpaste & brush
- Hand soap & shampoo
- Shaver
- Deodorant
- Prescription Meds
- 5-6 loose Band-Aids
- Fingernail clipper
- Hand/skin lotion

- Aleve or Advil (for pain)
- Aleve PM or Tylenol PM (sleep aid)
- Neosporin cream (antiseptic & soothe pain) or Gold Bond Medicated Pain & Itch Relief Cream
- Bactine 1st aid spray (relieves pain & itching, cuts, scrapes, burns)
- Kaopectate chews (anti-diarrhea)
- Milk of Magnesia chews (for constipation)
- Zicam, under tongue lozenge (take at the first sign of cold)
- Chloraseptic throat spray
- Alka-Seltzer Plus or Coricidin for colds
- Zyrtec – for allergies (the forest is full of pollens)

It seems like a lot of items. I have traveled for business for 40+ years, and there's nothing here I would leave out. All these items can be found in small-travel containers.

Items I pack for the fishing

- Two pairs of slacks (for fishing, fish cleaning, cooking, etc – when one pair gets too dirty I switch to the other.)
- One short sleeve polo shirt for each fishing day, plus 1-2 with long sleeves for colder days.
- A med-heavy weight sweater
- Underwear, T-shirts, and socks for each fishing day
- Hooded sweatshirt – for cooler days fishing (worn over a sweater, under rain gear)
- Rain suit – you want a good quality full rain suit…for protection in rain, wind, and cold…(with the raincoat large enough to

loosely fit over a sweater and hooded sweatshirt; with a hood large enough to keep your head dry, ample sleeve length; all comfortable to move and sit in. Try it out in the store – wear it for a period, move around – sit down in it. The rain suit's comfort and ability to work well are essential!

- We prefer the rain suit to be waterproof and breathable, and we prefer pants with suspenders rather than elastic waists (which never seem to work).

Note: Among your cabin gear, your rain suit should be packed last, on top of all else. You want it handy in case it rains on arrival day.

If you're going to spend money preparing for a Canadian fishing trip, I'd get two things…a **quality rain suit** and a **fishing reel with a smooth drag.**

- Rubber boots – of lighter weight, easy to get on and off. High enough to take a step into 6" of water. It seems like there's always water at the bottom of fishing boats. Rubber boots are welcome when getting in and out of a beached boat. But rubber boots can be clumsy, hot, and difficult for an old person to put on and take off. So, I skip the rubber boots and try to avoid the water. My outdoor shoes will dry in the evening next to the heater.

- Gloves – this gets tricky – finding gloves light enough to operate fishing reels…and warm enough for cold days. I've tried latex surgical gloves, but I didn't find them to work as well as I hoped. On colder days, I now use yellow farmer gloves and slip them off when needed. Yes, they get wet during the day. They dry on the cabin heater in the evening. (They do provide some protection from being poked by fish fins.)

- Hat – My dermatologist and I like a wide brim that provides sun protection on all sides of my head... and aids in shedding rain. I wear it under my rain jacket hood. You want an under-chinstrap for those breezy trips across the lake. Those of us with tours of Vietnam service appreciate the Boonie hat. (I'm sorry, caps provide too little protection.)

- Stocking cap – perfect for cold mornings (yes, in the boat, I take both the Boonie hat and stocking cap)

- Light down jacket/vest – (optional) for just a little extra warmth versus wearing the rain jacket...while fishing, around the cabin, taking a hike, or walking to the lodge for dinner...a medium-weight down jacket is just right. You may tie it on top of your travel duffle

- Bath towels. The camps will provide ample bedding (sheets and blankets) but usually not bath towels. So, we automatically pack a couple of our bath towels per person. We also take 1-2 scrap towels for general use – having one in the boat is handy!

- Pillow – I've shared how I now pack my own, comfortable pillow. It's welcome in the cabin – and in the vehicle's back seat.

Forced to leave...
We had made two portages to get to the desired lake (we were

Chapter 5 – What Do We Pack?

younger). Fishing was slow in the morning, but the fishing was suddenly better in the afternoon as the weather worsened. In those days, we had cheap, crappy rain gear – and as much as we enjoyed the fishing activity – the more the rain fell, the colder we became. It was not a threatening storm, just a COLD rain.

We became so chilled that we were forced to give up the super fishing and re-trace our way back to the cabin. We were upset with ourselves. We swore it was our last trip without quality rain gear.

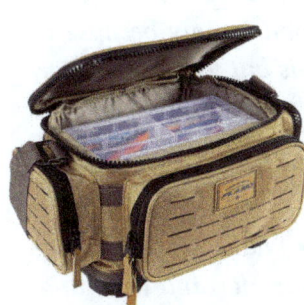

What I pack for the boat

- Tackle boxes/bags

I like taking my soft-side tackle bag in the boat. It holds a lot, is well organized, and doesn't tip over easily. My soft-side tackle bag is smaller…14" long, 10" wide, and 10" high – with pockets everywhere. I've never wished for it to be larger.

I bring a larger hard-side tackle box (simply because I have it), with more lures, sinkers, spare reels, extra line, light repair tools, reel oil, and crap I'll never use. I draw from it in the evenings - resupplying the smaller tackle bag. This larger tackle box stays in the cabin.

I'm not going to get into fishing methods and tactics, but I want to share that a person doesn't need a lot of tackle. Most of our days are devoted to fishing for walleye; 75% of our fishing is with a minnow (or Berkley Gulp with curly tail) on a lead head jig (jigging while slowly back trolling or drifting). Of course, we have a gazillion jigs in various weights and colors (bright pink, white, yellow….)

Then, we carry a few lures for trolling or casting for northern pike and bass, especially jointed-floating Rapala's, Jigging Raps, and the Canadian-made **Williams Wabler** spoons. One of our

guides taught us to use at least 18" steel leaders when fishing northern pike. Shorter ones aren't long enough.

My dear neighbor Don, who fished Canada 4-5 times each summer, bought a Williams Wabler spoon mainly because it was on sale. He'd often fished with spoons but was unfamiliar with this brand. After the first day of fishing and seeing the Williams Wabler's results, those in his group begged him to sell it – the bidding got to $25.

On one of our trips, I loaned a Williams Wabler to one in our group. He had just snapped it onto his leader and cast, and immediately said, 'Oh no, it's snagged.' We looked at the area where he'd cast, and suddenly, a giant northern pike cleared the water with the Wabler in its mouth. We all laughed and together said, "That's not a snag."

In the soft tackle bag going to the boat

- Fishing license & Outdoors Card (in plastic Ziplock)
- Lake map (in plastic Ziplock)
- Compass
- Lures, hooks, swivels, sinkers, leaders, packaged bait, etc. (for the species you're after)
- Fish stringer (of stout rope, no metal clips)

- Scissors or clipper
- Pocket knife
- Fillet knife
- Kitchen scissors (handy for fish cleaning, like cutting through tough fish skin)
- Hook sharpener
- Sunglasses
- Bug spray
- Suntan lotion
- Band-aids
- Firelighter
- 2-way radios
- Billfold and cell phone in plastic Ziplock
- Long-nosed pliers, forceps, or a medical hemostat are perfect for removing fish hooks from the mouth of an angry northern pike. You once had to know a nurse to obtain a used **hemostat** - they're now sold in fishing stores. We like for the hemostat joint to be near the jaw end and the jaws to be short and straight, all to get a stronger grip on fish hooks. Fishing guides clip their hemostat to the front of your rain jacket – a mark of their profession.

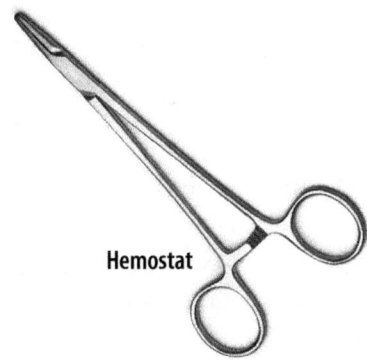
Hemostat

We prefer to pack our tackle bags/boxes in one of the cargo totes for transport, to protect them.

Fishing poles
We suggest bringing 2-3 per person, 6½-7 foot 'medium-heavy' action graphite rods. (Lighter action rods are fine for pan fish, but they're just too wimpy for this fishing.)

The Canadian Fishing Adventure

We purchase two-part graphite rods. In our mind, they have 99% of the delicate 'feel' people want from one-piece rods, and they're far easier to transport (especially if you're flying). I take two rods in the boat daily and usually have another in the cabin as a spare.

Reels

We prefer open-face spinning reels and pack at least two. You'll want good, rugged reels with a quality line drag that smoothly applies friction with a 3-4 pound load.

The drag applies some tension to the line when a fish is pulling… but not so much, hopefully, where the line breaks. The reel doesn't need to be expensive (some are crazy high-priced.) But it is essential that the drag works smoothly! Even medium-sized Canadian fish will put a test on your rod and reel.

There are enough ways to lose a great catch – let's control what we can.

To us, open-face spinning reels are more comfortable to hold and operate (versus top-mounted casting reels.) You have the rod and reel in one grasp with your dominant hand (if you're right-handed, you'll hold it with your right hand…and turn the crank with your left hand.) The crank can be switched to the other side if you're left-handed.

Chapter 5 – What Do We Pack?

The reel weight hangs under the rod, providing a balanced feel and making dealing with a fighting lunker easier.

Depth finder (one per boat)
The world now has fantastic fish finders…live color video, forward view, side view, 360 view, and chart plotter; lordy, they might even prepare shore lunch. But they can cost thousands! I've not used a fish locator in this league – but we know people who swear by them; the technology works. If you're one to go this route, good for you; we do not argue.

We use a more basic $120 depth finder to see the water depth – and the bottom structure. When we've been catching fish in 15ft of water and look down to see it's suddenly 25ft deep…we quickly move back to shallower water. It's as simple as that.

The key component on all fish-depth finders is the transducer. It sits in the water, pointed down. You want to mount it so it's in the water pointed down when the boat is stopped or moving slowly…but out of the way of rushing water when your boat is at speed.

To avoid damaging the delicate transponder, one must be careful while docking and beaching. Ours has a secondary cord to tie it off in case its suction cup comes loose – the cord has saved the day more than once.

Remember to pack the charger. Our fish-depth finder needs recharging each day, so we take it to the cabin at night, along with the rods, reels, and tackle bag. Lord knows what can happen to items left in the boat at night – we'd just as soon not find out.

Dip nets, minnow buckets, and boat seats with a back
We're going to assume your fishing camp provides a fish dip net and a minnow bucket for each boat – along with boat seats with

backs – if not, you'll want to. It's handy not having to pack those items.

Life jacket – personal floatation device.
Most camps do NOT provide a life jacket – you'll need to bring one that fits you.

I've used two styles: a combination life jacket/fishing vest with lots of pockets and a little extra warmth. I never found it as handy as it looked for fishing from a boat. It was somewhat 'bulky,' so I usually had it off while fishing in the boat, and if I'd placed something in a pocket, I'd later find myself forgetting where I'd put it. They're probably ideal for standing in a river, or fishing from shore.

I now prefer the self-inflating type – if you fall in the water, it automatically inflates. Or, you can pull the tab to inflate it. They're less cumbersome. I wear it when running at speed in the boat or when wind and waves become concerning, and while fishing by myself.

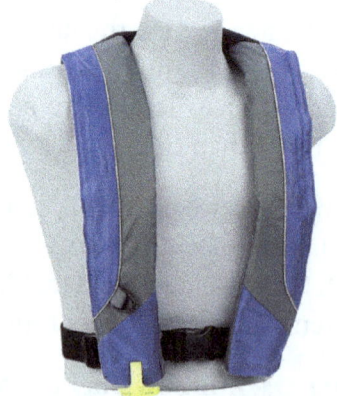

Chapter 5 – What Do We Pack?

Sad story...
I met a fellow who had just returned from a week fishing in Manitoba. He shared a terrible experience. He said he and a friend were transiting the lake at speed when he believed they struck something, causing both to be thrown from the boat. Neither was wearing a life jacket.

Now both in the water, the fellow sharing the story noticed his partner was unconscious and sinking. He shared how he tried his best to hold his friend above water but could not.

He shared how the boat continued slowly in circles, and he tried repeatedly to grab it as it passed. After several passes, he could finally grasp a hold – but by then, he lacked the strength to pull himself back onboard.

At this point, the other boat in their group—now about ¼ mi ahead—noticed the situation and turned to help. After much struggle, the second boat was able to get the survivor into its boat.

Hours later, the camp operator and local officials located their deceased friend.

Water-tight 'utility bag'
This solution came to us out of necessity and it's proven so handy! A rugged, water-tight bag about the size of a garbage can. We found ours in an Army surplus store…a light canvas outer layer with a rubberized inner layer. (The Army-Navy stores call it a rubberized waterproof laundry bag, $10.)

As the day warms up, you need a dry place to put layers of apparel you're shedding. This bag is just the place. Its waterproof liner is perfect for sitting at the bottom of a camp boat in an inch of water. One utility bag holds the items from three of us. A large trash bag is the right size but too easily torn.

In the bottom of our 'utility bag,' we always have:
- A small first-aid kit
- 25' length of rope
- A roll of duct tape
- A flashlight
- An 8' x 10' poly tarp folded for protection from wind & rain during shore lunches
- And a sealed plastic bag holding 20-30 sheets of paper towel for fire starter, toilet paper, etc.
- And a scrap towel

All the items have been called upon more than once!

Items to pack for the Cabin:
- Paper towels, 2-3 rolls if you're cooking
- Trash bags, box of 30 large size
- Disposable drinking glasses for cocktails, etc.
- Kleenex
- 4 x 6" notepad and pen for reminder notes, 'boat checklist,' etc.
- Sharpie pen for writing on freezer bags
- Bug spray
- Bottled water

The water in most fishing camps is potable (approved for

drinking), but you'll likely find it stained by tannins from the forest – often the color of iced tea. When you add whiskey to the water, it becomes dark coffee in appearance. We'll wash dishes and bathe in the camp water, but we prefer bottled water for drinking, cooking, ice cubes, and making coffee.

You can consider how much you'll need. We'd take one well-wrapped case of water in bottles (like this pictured) for three of us for five days, and more if we're making coffee.

When available, we'll use ice from the camp's ice machine, which is usually well-filtered.

- **Two extension cords with multi-plug-in adapters** to charge digital devices, depth finders, possibly a fan or two, and who knows what else.

- **Small electric fan.** A favorite of ours for the warmer days but, not so enjoyed by the generator-powered camps. We'll close up the cabin, pull the shades and turn on a small fan (or two). It's so welcome.

- **11W LED bulb.** Many camps use low-wattage bulbs in their cabins to minimize the power drain from generators. We'll bring a somewhat brighter, low-energy LED bulb to switch out for our stay – it makes reading and playing cards easier.

Items to pack if you're cooking meals in the cabin

- quality utility knife
- quality metal spatula
- pair quality kitchen hot mitts
- quality can opener
- full size non-stick fry pan

The camps have plates, bowls, utensils, pots, and pans for

preparing meals. When we cook in the cabin, we will use some of their kitchen items…but we've also found taking a few trusted items of our own to be helpful. We mark these items as ours – and remember to repack them when we leave.

2-3 rolls of paper towels

Dishwashing rag & drying towels

Copy of the planned menu – and recipes if necessary

Salt & pepper

Freezer zip-lock plastic bags. (one box, 1-gal size) For freezing walleyes and waterproofing items – like lake maps, cell phones, and two-way radios.

One zip-lock bag with ½ cup of flour, (or desired fish breading) for each planned shore lunch.

Coffee
A hot cup of coffee will be welcome early in the morning – both in the cabin or from a thermos out on the lake on a chilly, rainy day. How coffee is made available should be one of your early questions to prospective camps.

You'll likely prepare coffee at a drive-in camp, much like at home. But, at generator-powered camps (fly-in and boat-in), they will likely prepare coffee for you in the lodge. We love the camps that bring a canister of hot coffee to your cabin early in the morning, (we are getting spoiled.)

If you're asked to prepare coffee in your cabin, the camp will likely have a stovetop percolator for you to use. You'll need to bring the coffee and filters. If coffee is important (and it is to us), you can pack a quality stovetop percolator. Coleman makes a 12-

Chapter 5 – What Do We Pack?

cup percolator (shown here) that would be good for indoor and outdoor coffee brewing.

First thing in the morning, we brew a pot to drink as we wake up, and with breakfast, and then we brew another pot to fill the thermoses.

- Grocery items – when you're cooking meals in your cabin

We have the designated cook put together a menu for each meal well in advance of the trip. This is prepared and shared with group members weeks in advance of our departure, sticking to choices the cook is comfortable preparing. Doing this in advance allows us to identify food likes/dislikes, diet issues, and insert some variety between meals, while omitting the meals we plan to have a shore lunch or eat in the lodge.

It looks something like this:

Monday

Breakfast: fried eggs, bacon, toast, orange juice, coffee

Lunch: (Shore Lunch), walleye, fried potatoes, asparagus

Dinner: In Lodge

Tuesday

Breakfast: scrambled eggs, sausage links, toast, orange juice, coffee

Lunch: (Shore Lunch), walleye, green beans, canned peaches

Dinner: Tomato soup, grilled cheese sandwiches, tossed salad

Wednesday

Breakfast: cheese omelets, sausage patties, toast, orange juice, coffee

Lunch: (Shore Lunch), cheeseburgers, potato chips, canned peaches

Dinner: Beef stew (canned), rice, green beans, toast

We'd suggest sticking to simple menu choices, ideally prepared on the stovetop, rather than using the oven. Ideally, it may be as simple as opening a couple of cans and heating. Because of the generated electricity, camps usually do not have microwaves.

Once the menu is established, picture each grocery item needed for each meal. For instance, for the above Monday breakfast of fried eggs, bacon, toast, orange juice, coffee:

- 2 eggs for each person
- 2-3 strips of bacon per person
- 2 slices of bread each, browned in a frying pan. Pre-butter the bread, like making grill cheese sandwiches. Generator camps won't have electric toasters.
- butter
- 1 orange juice container per person
- coffee with desired additions (sugar, dairy)
- salt and pepper

The morning preparation plan

First, start the coffee.

Next, with our non-stick fry pan, fry the bacon first, then the eggs.

Ask a group member to brown some bread – using a stove top burner and frying pan.

Have another member set out an orange juice container for each person, butter, salt, pepper, and paper towels for napkins.

We do as much food prepping in advance as possible. For instance, for a cheeseburger lunch, we'd purchase pre-made

Chapter 5 – What Do We Pack?

hamburger patties; our orange juice and tomato juice are in individual cartons; and flour is pre-added to baggies – ready for each lunch's fish filets.

Each individual is asked to bring the snack item(s) they prefer, with enough to share. (Peanuts, M&M's, Snickers, and summer sausage and cheese with crackers are all popular.)

We doubt there's anyone who makes this trip to cook. But with some planning and sharing of duties, meal prep goes smoothly and doesn't need to be hard on anyone.

We've found it best not to share the cooking, but for others to aid the cook (finding items, setting out items, washing dishes, wiping down countertops, etc.). Multiple cooks can get confusing.

We work to keep meal preparations simple. Each breakfast is basically the same, with a different meat or egg preparation for variation (sunny side up, scrambled, omelets, etc.). We'll have fried walleye shore lunch each noon, interrupted with one lunch of cheeseburgers or chili dogs. If we must prepare our own evening meal, we use stove-top entree choices like:

Sloppy Joes

Hamburger/macaroni goulash

One pot spaghetti

Chili

Chili dogs

Cheeseburgers

Tacos

Southwestern beef & rice

Shrimp & pasta skillet

Grilled/fried pork chops, with boxed au gratin potatoes and canned peas

Hamburger vegetable soup*

Tuna & noodles

Hamburger-potato skillet

Mac & cheese w/ bologna

Chicken chow mein w/ rice

The above Hamburger Vegetable Soup is a hearty and flavorful one-pot meal. It's a favorite.

Terry Leininger, the author's cousin, shares his recipe. (Terry is a retired Navy Senior Master Chief and avid fisherman!)

*Hamburger Vegetable Soup – from Terry Leininger
Ingredients:
   1 pound lean ground beef

   1 pound sausage

   1 onion diced

   2 cloves garlic, minced

   medium potatoes, peeled and diced

   3 cups mixed vegetables, fresh or frozen

   3½ cups beef broth

   canned diced tomatoes with juice, 28 ounces

   1 can condensed tomato soup

   2 teaspoons Worcestershire sauce

   1 teaspoon Italian seasoning

   1 bay leaf

   salt and pepper to taste

Chapter 5 – What Do We Pack?

Instructions:
Brown onion, ground beef, sausage, onion, and garlic until no pink remains. Drain fat. Add the other ingredients and simmer covered for 10-15 mins.

If you're fixing your evening meal the first day, you can get your kitchen items in order – and start with the menu choice for the first night. It's nice having it planned – with the needed grocery items on hand.

If you're eating in the lodge the first evening, great, you just finish your cocktail and walk up to the lodge, greeting the other guests and enjoy what we've always found to be terrific meals.

It's always a surprise to enter a fishing lodge, hours from home, and run into someone you know – or a neighbor to someone we know. It's such a small world. But, we're getting ahead of ourselves. Once your group, especially the cook, has decided upon the menu, he or she can list the necessary grocery items.

At our local grocery store (in the US), we'll purchase canned and non-refrigerated packaged items like pasta, canned beans, canned soups, vegetables, and cooking oil. Grocery items are packed in a separate kitchen box, which may be kept in the cabin's kitchen area.

Fresh-perishable items, like meats, fresh vegetables, milk, cheese, juices, eggs, and bread are purchased in Canada. We pick a grocery store in one of the last towns we pass through en route to our fishing camp.

The Canadian grocery stores we've experienced are much like those in the US. They are modern, well-stocked, and helpful. They will gladly 'box' your purchases for more accessible transport into your camp. Have a handy trash bag to protect the grocery box should it rain.

The Canadian Fishing Adventure

Checklist
We include our complete **Packing Checklist** on page 133 for you to copy and serve as a start for your own list.

Take your fly-fishing gear
My son Scott took along his fly rod and a few mouse-like flies one year. He wanted to see what catching a northern pike on a fly rod would be like.

After just one or two casts from the camp's boat dock – a real nice Northern was hooked, and the battle began. My son and I were laughing. Others in the camp came down to watch and cheer.

After a struggle and running for a dip net...a dandy 35" northern pike was landed and released.

A fellow in camp was heard saying, 'That looked like such fun. I'm bringing my fly rod next trip!' Fly fishing for northern pike took off at that camp—and I'm afraid we may be to blame.

CHAPTER 5 – WHAT DO WE PACK?

An Umbrella?
If your trip is scheduled when the weather could be hotter, consider a portable boat umbrella to ward off the hot sun. I've fished on such days, and even with a broad-brimmed hat, I would have given anything for a bit of overhead shade.

Adjustable umbrellas like this clamp onto a seat or hull and can be quickly moved aside when a fish bites. They're cheap enough, so it's no big deal if something happens to them.

Yes, your buddies will laugh. Then, an hour into a hot sunny afternoon, they'll be begging to use it.

Take your dog along
Canada makes it easy if you're among the many who would enjoy having your dog join you.

First, Buddy needs a rabies vaccine within the last year – with a veterinarian certificate sharing the dog's identifying features, the vaccine's trade name, serial number, and duration. In addition, the pet needs to appear healthy. If not, an added 'health inspection' can be required.

Some Canadian provinces prohibit certain dog breeds. For instance, Ontario does not allow 'pit bull-type' dogs. So, if your dog could be confused with a pit bull, have your veterinarian provide a document describing its pedigree stating otherwise – or leave Buddy home.

Canada allows up to 44 lbs of US commercially packaged pet food, unopened. It is only to be eaten by your pet while in Canada.

THE CANADIAN FISHING ADVENTURE

To reenter the US, Buddy must just appear healthy. Coming from Canada, he/she does not need proof of Rabi's vaccine. You can re-enter the US with up to 50 pounds of pet food (not containing lamb, sheep, or goat meat, with clearly labeled ingredients) in an unopened commercial package – manufactured in the US or Canada.

You'll want to inquire how welcome Buddy will be at your fishing destination and lodging sites along the way.

Chapter 5 – What Do We Pack?

Marabou jigs for sale...
One evening after a day of fishing, we were having an adult beverage in the camp lodge – we noticed sitting behind the bar, a collection of feathered jigs hanging from a glass – with a 75 cents sign. So, I purchased several. They'd been made by one of their guides, an Indigenous Canadian.

That winter, I thought I'd try to do the same thing myself. I purchased and painted the lead head jigs and the colored feathers. We learned that when it comes to tying lures, they are called Marabou feathers – which sounds classy. Otherwise, they're just domestic turkey feathers.

Anyway, my young sons and I had fun painting and tying different-colored Marabou jigs. Over the winter, we made several dozen.

The next June, en route to Canada with our regular group, I shared how I had made quite a few jigs and would be glad to share some. Of course, one of the fellows questioned my skills – adding that the Indian guides imparted critical secret techniques when making their jigs.

So, the first afternoon out fishing, I anxiously tied on my best-hand-tied jig...and added a minnow. It hardly had time to get wet when WHAM. It was a nice three-pound walleye. As it neared the boat, I said, "Gentlemen, the price of jigs just went up!"

CHAPTER 6

First Hours in Camp

When first in camp, however we arrived, fly-in, boat-in or drive-in, we're always in a rush to go fishing, but a few things you might consider.

The camp staff will likely get your gear to the step outside your cabin.

Unpacking grocery items
Let's first unpack the grocery items that need refrigeration. The cook is best to do this – he/she will need to know where things are placed.

One person can prepare a sandwich for each person. Cold meat or peanut butter/jelly are good choices, just for simplicity. Place the sandwiches in a small Igloo cooler with beverages, snacks, and candy bars. That will be today's lunch out on the lake.

Fishing license
If the camp provides fishing licenses, share your driver's license and Outdoor Card with the camp operator, and they will prepare your license. I place the license and Outdoor Card in a small Ziplock at the bottom of my tackle bag, where they can't blow out. (Available if a game warden checks while we're on the lake.)

Pick a bed
Throw your duffle on a bed that looks good for you. That'll be your home for the week.

Change into your fishing apparel
Change into your fishing clothes if you're still in your traveling apparel. As you dress, remember it's usually cooler on the water, so pack an extra layer or two in the utility bag. Make your rain gear one of the layers.

I usually take my billfold and cell phone with me in the boat. They're both placed in a Ziplock bag in the tackle bag. The billfold won't be needed on the lake, but it's with me. You'll likely not receive cell service, but the phone's camera and GPS features can be handy. And I hate leaving those items in the cabin.

Unpack and assemble rods and reels
Get the rods out of the rod tube, assemble them, attach the reels, string line through the guides, and rig up the desired tackle you wish to start with. I prepare two rods with somewhat different rigs (like...one with a favorite jig and one with a spinner rig). I leave a spare rod in the cabin with my larger tackle box.

Several non-fishing tackle items important to have in your tackle bag: several band aids, sunglasses, suntan lotion, bug lotion, and the lake map (and GPS device).

Is the boat ready?
Make one individual in the group responsible for preparing the boat(s) for each outing...Is the gas tank full? Does the motor start? Are there oars? Has water been dipped out?

Add minnows in the minnow buckets. We find it handy to use two of the camp's minnow buckets per boat: one tied where it's convenient for the person running the motor...and the second tied mid-way down the opposite side for the others to access. For the afternoon, we would start with two dozen minnows per person.

At the end of the fishing day, if there are still minnows…we'll tie the minnow buckets to the boat's transom (rear) so they'll remain in the water and not drag in sand or bang rocks. If several minnows die while fishing or at night, we'll still fish with them. They're costly.

Some minnow bucket lids have a locking device – it's best to take advantage of this and lock the lids closed in the evenings. Raccoons are clever little critters known to clean out the minnows during the night hours.

> *Minnow delivery to Northwoods camps is an interesting business. Visualize a float plane pilot seining minnows from an isolated pond and then transporting them in oxygen-filled plastic globes in their aircraft. The pilots announce their arrival at camps by low-level buzzing of the lodge – landing and quickly transferring the live bait to the camp's aerated tanks – all coincidentally just in time for lunch.*

Canada does not allow the import of live bait from the US. We've fished with Canadian nightcrawlers and leeches, and find minnows work best, followed by Berkley Gulp.

Gear for the boat
In the cabin, start setting your gear out to carry to the boat. Hopefully, the depth finder is charged. Use the *'For the boat'* checklist (repeated here) to ensure you have what's needed. We won't have shore lunch this first afternoon, so those items can be skipped.

- Life jackets

- Tackle bag/box
- Depth finder
- Rods – reels
- Sandwich lunches & snacks – (when not having a shore lunch)
- Beverage cooler, w/ice, water, drinks
- Utility bag for apparel
- Sunglasses

Add for shore lunch:
- Fish filets – if cleaned the evening before
- Zip-lock with flour
- Cooking oil
- Salt & pepper
- Thermos w/coffee

A water spout!
On one trip, we were in our usual mad rush to begin fishing the first afternoon; it was a lovely sunny day...and we didn't even think about taking our rain gear. As the afternoon went on, a dark storm quickly approached from the west – we were several miles from camp, too far to dash in. But we hoped the storm would pass to one side or the other (Yah, right.)

Suddenly, the fast-approaching front wall of the storm turned solid white in intense rain...and, of course, wind. We looked to the left of our two boats to see a perfectly formed water spout – a water-based tornado about 150 yards away.

We turned for the shore only 20 yards away, as the wind forced us in that direction anyway. The shoreline was a vertical two-

foot edge of tree roots. We slowly drove the boat against the shore, grounding on underwater sand.

Of course, the wind-driven rain quickly soaked us. We had brought our utility bag (which we use to hold clothing as we shed layers of clothing during the day). In the bag, we keep an 8'x10' poly tarp. We quickly got the tarp out, and the three of us in our boat crudely used the tarp to gain some protection.

About as quickly as the storm started, it passed. We were drenched and cold. We abandoned fishing for the afternoon, dragging ourselves back to camp to dry off.

Sitting on our cabin's deck with a welcome cocktail, we watched other fishermen-women casually pulling in at day's end. The brunt of the storm had not hit them, and...they had remembered their rain gear.

Two free northern pike
Four of us were spending a week at an Ontario fly-in camp. I was delighted to have my outdoor-loving son, an avid fishing fan, joining us. He'd flown from California for the outing – so I hoped the fishing would not disappoint. After the morning's short float plane flight into camp and our usual mad rush to get on the lake, our two boats headed to an area we thought might prove successful (some of us had fished these waters before.) Rigged up with jigs with minnows, we'd hardly put them in the water, and WHAM, we had a walleye on...and WHAM... another. The other boat, about 50 yards away, was doing just as well. We were all laughing.

Our success was far from over. My son and I often had two walleyes on at once, so we'd had to handle the dip net ourselves.

Then, to simplify the process, we skipped the dip net and grabbed the hooked walleye with our hands (by reaching for the lead head of the jig.)

Then, WHAM, just as I reached for the jig head, a sizeable northern pike (mouth full of teeth!) grabbed the fish across the trunk of its body... inches from my fingers. Lordy. And refused to let go. So now, with a walleye AND a large northern on the line, we used the dip net to lift both fish out. Lying in the bottom of the boat, the northern pike continued to hold the walleye.

A few minutes later, this happened again – and thankfully again, my fingers escaped injury. The Northerns must have centered on the school of walleyes we'd encountered. And those walleyes we caught and had struggling beside the boat were viewed as easy prey. No wonder the walleyes seemed anxious to get out of the water.

We released all but two or three of the walleyes, enough for shore lunch the next day. We kept the two northern pike; they were cleaned, frozen, and taken home. Their fillets and their story were shared with others.

That evening, my son asked if fishing at this camp was always as good. We laughed and said, 'Fishing's good in Canada, this afternoon topped the list!' I was glad he enjoyed himself.

CHAPTER 7

Finally, Out on the Lake

Taking care…
We all want to return from a day fishing without serious incidents. During a day on the lakes we fish, we MAY see 1-2 other boats, and they're likely at a distance. We enjoy the low fishing pressure and solitude – that's what we wanted – but we're well aware that if we should run into 'trouble', help is going to take a while to arrive.

It's our experience that there are several ways fishermen can get into trouble…

Boating in poor weather
Let's start with high winds. No fish are worth the dangers and ordeal of fighting waves and wind. Stay in the cabin, and enjoy your book. If the wind increases during the day, you'd better head in. We've sometimes waited too long and endured pounding and scary rides transiting lakes.

This brief YouTube video provides helpful tips for operating a fishing boat in rough waters:

>   https://www.youtube.com/watch?v=trsKPuglnoM

While out on the water, an approaching storm is easy to observe. Some storms will skirt around; some pass harmlessly overhead…

so we usually continue fishing, watching the storm's progress. However, we have our eye on a protected shoreline where we could run when needed. And if necessary – beach the boat and hunker down on shore. (Remember the 8'x10' tarp.) Most rain storms last only 30-60 minutes.

If the storm produces lightning, don't delay, the US Forest Service recommends:

- Immediately lay down your fishing rods (they act like lightning rods).
- Head to the nearest shore & beach the boat.
- Disperse yourselves at least 100 yards from the shore and 30 feet from each other – so not everyone will be struck at once.
- You can 'hunker down', but remain on your feet. Don't lay or sit on the ground (less area in contact with the ground).
- Avoid the tallest trees or standing immediately next to a tree if you're in a forested area.

Getting indoors is a far better strategy…like an abandoned cabin or a cabin's porch. We'd run back to the camp – but that's usually more than an hour away.

They felt like stones…
One afternoon, in a sunny blue sky, a lone thunderstorm approached. We continued fishing, keeping an eye on the storm's path – and headed for a winding, narrow river, where we'd be protected from wind and waves.

The small storm started with a blast of wind and driving rain – we were glad to be wearing good rain gear. The wind settled down only to be replaced by hail. Thankfully, there was no lightning. (Those of us working in offices aren't used to being outside in such conditions.)

Chapter 7 – Finally, Out on the Lake

While the narrow river sheltered us from waves, the hail was different – the boat's bottom was quickly covered with hailstones. And they felt like stones through our rain gear. I turned to see how my son in the front of the boat was doing… and laughed at what I saw. He's much brighter than his dad… and was holding an old life preserver-seat cushion over his head to ward off the hail. What a good idea – I immediately copied him.

The storm passed in 30 minutes, and we were back fishing, with a new tale to share.

Striking underwater objects

You'll be boating in water that is probably unfamiliar to you. When fishing at idle speeds, usually back trolling, we don't give much concern to bumping into underwater objects – logs or rocks. When transiting across the water at speed, all should be watchful for objects above or just under the surface.

Camp operators often mark serious underwater obstructions, like reefs, underwater islands, and submerged rocks, with a float – especially obstructions on passageways where fishermen are likely to transit at speed. But it's hard to mark them all; sometimes the floats move…and the obstruction might have a mate.

While underway in unfamiliar water, it's wise to choose a speed less than full ramming speed – just in case. We have struck underwater rocks in the middle of open bays – thank goodness we had only a 15 hp motor, so our speed was reduced. But it's still jarring. People will be thrown forward. In one case, the impact caused a spark plug wire to come off the spark plug. Thankfully, no one was injured, and no harm was done to the hull or motor.

We've found it doesn't matter if a lake has high or low water when we're there. It's just a different set of obstructions that become a threat. Just take it easy with the speed – and be watchful.

Getting lost
We love irregularly shaped lakes with islands, bays, points, etc. One concern with such waters is remaining oriented. The shoreline of large islands looks just like regular terrain.

Imagine you've been trolling along for a couple of hours, concentrating on your fishing and enjoying the day, and someone asks, *'Where are we?'*

Let's start with how we keep from getting lost when fishing unfamiliar lakes.

In the weeks before departing home, we obtain a quality map of the lake system we plan to fish.

You're looking for a map with detail, something like 1:24,000 scale (1 inch of map = ⅓ mile on the ground; lower than 24,000 is better).

Your camp operator may have such maps available, or you can check if one of these Canadian map sources has your lake: Expect to pay for a quality map.

https://findamap.mytopo.com/findamap

https://geohub.lio.gov.on.ca/datasets/mnrf::historic-bathymetry-maps

http://www.canadamapsales.com/en/catalogue/AnglingMaps/

You're looking for a map showing small details, like the odd shape of a small island or the river's curve and how it enters the lake at the side of a small bay. These are the peculiarities that help you identify your position.

Immediately, as the boat pulls away from camp, the map reader

Chapter 7 – Finally, Out on the Lake

in your group turns the map so the direction you're going is the top as you hold it. Put your finger on your position as you move away from camp.

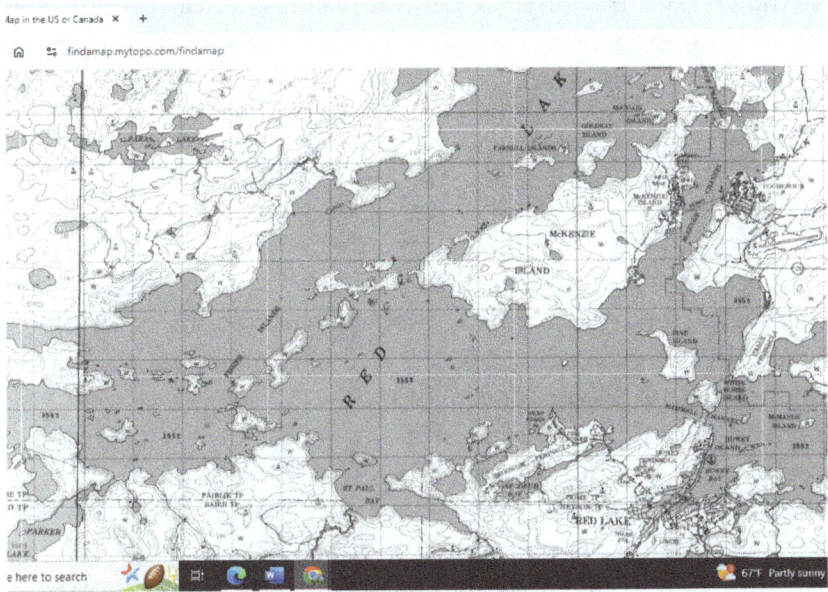

Notice the shoreline passing by – how the real-life features are somewhat mirrored on the map. Note how a small pointed island passing on the left is also displayed on the map.

Most aircraft pilots who navigate by watching the features on the ground (called pilotage) become lost in the first miles of their journey.

When it's cloudy or foggy, you'll want to exercise extra caution to avoid being 'turned around.' If you become disoriented…first relax and take a breath.

Then try this: Get out your compass (a quality field compass). Now, align yourself, the boat, and the map so that they all point north (north is the top of 99% of maps).

Now look around at your nearby shoreline features, like two small islands, one a bit larger, aligned close to the larger shoreline, or a point extending out from the right side of a small bay…etc. If you've been tracking your travel progress until recently, you know the basic area you're in – so you have an idea of the general area on the map to start.

If nothing matches up, travel 2-300 yards and try it again. (Boat, map, and compass all pointed north)

Another exercise may prove interesting. On day one, open your map, find your camp, and then position the map's shoreline to align with the real shoreline. Now, lay your compass on top of where the camp is identified and turn the compass so its case aligns with the compass needle… both pointing magnetic north. Now, draw a faint pencil line arrow on the map – over the camp's location – representing the direction of 'magnetic north' at that spot. You'll see how magnetic north relates to the top of the map. (There will be some angle of difference.)

Most quality lake maps are quite large. Before heading out, we'll fold the map in the cabin so the area we're traveling in that day is the upper fold. Then, we place it face up in a large Ziplock bag. It gets held and viewed often. Be careful it doesn't blow out of the boat when underway.

When we were new to fishing expansive Northwoods lakes, we would keep our journeys closer to camp. You can troll along one shore for a few hours and then reverse your path trolling back.

CHAPTER 7 – FINALLY, OUT ON THE LAKE

GPS assistance

Is there a place for digital tools like GPS (global positioning system) to track where we are while fishing among islands and bays?

I contacted my son, who's used these devices to track his location while fishing mountain lakes and hunting in deserts. His opening comment was, 'They work great when they work!'

He shares two formats of GPS assistance to consider…

The first and cheapest option is to add a GPS mapping application to your cell phone. Although there is no cell service in most of the Northwoods, thankfully, that's not needed to access satellite-based GPS signals.

He recommends the Gaia GPS application. Go to gaiafps.com to open an account (there's a free version), then download the app from the Apple App Store or Google Play Store. We recommend doing this to check it out.

Once you're comfortable with Gaia GPS, you'll need to download the map(s) of the Canadian lake area where you plan to fish. You may access these through Gaia GPS or a Canadian map source, like Canada Topo or Backroad Mapbooks.

More maps are available with the 'Premium' version of Gaia GPS (which is only $40 per year.) Downloading the overlaying maps must be done while you have cell or wi-fi service.

With the correct map overlay and everything else working, this format will provide your current location and a 'breadcrumb' trail of your path – leading you back to camp. You'll want to gain comfort operating this format before leaving home.

Our second digital option is for you to purchase a dedicated **handheld GPS device**, of which Garmin and other sources offer a gazillion models. These devices are more rugged and somewhat simpler to operate than the cell phone-based choice – but also a bit more costly.

Here, we chose the Garmin model **GPSMAP 67i** to describe the features and capabilities available. This device displays your current location on the map, a track of the path you took to that point, and with a subscription service, you have emergency SOS service (voice or text with Garmin's 24-hour response center, who then alert nearby assistance) and two-way messaging – and weather information.

This device costs $500 – 600, depending on the source, and has various subscription options, starting at $30 initially and $12 / mo. We understand the messaging – SOS service subscription can be suspended for periods when the device is not in use.

Chapter 7 – Finally, Out on the Lake

This model is among the upper end of Garmin's handhelds; others with fewer features and smaller screens are less expensive.

On our next Canada fishing trip, we plan to use the Gaia GPS app on our cell phone, in conjunction with a quality paper map.

We appreciate the wider view that printed maps provide – useful for planning and considering options, which can be difficult on the smaller screens of cellphones and GPS devices. In the evenings, we enjoy laying out the printed map on the cabin's kitchen table and discussing the next day's travels, plus, they don't require recharging.

Back to getting in trouble…
While we fuel the boat's gas tanks and get minnows each morning, we share with the camp operator which lake area we plan to fish that day, so they'll be aware.

Fish camp's rental outboards are fuel efficient – remember to have the camp operators re-fill the gas tanks each morning. You'll have hours of run time, especially if you've just been trolling most of the day. You should have plenty of gas to find your way to familiar waters.

If you still find yourself 'turned around' after using the above navigational resources – or your boat or motor has an issue… and you find yourself running out of daylight, we'd suggest pulling onto a beach or a protected area for the boat. An island might help in avoiding larger wildlife. Gather firewood and build a fire. Prepare a shelter using the vinyl tarp. You're probably going to be spending the night there. Your absence won't be noted until later in the evening – or the following day.

While sheltered up on shore, you might just as well fish a little – and consider a shore supper. Your camp operator will come by boat or float plane looking for you in the morning. You'll be OK – and have quite the story.

> *Out of the fog…*
> *While fishing at a fly-in lake one sunny morning, we encountered a fog bank. At first, we thought it was fun – certainly different. After only a few minutes, we had no idea which direction we were going.*
>
> *We continued trolling for a period – with growing concern, when out of the fog, we came across two small white buoys. We were familiar with this part of the lake and suddenly knew where we were. These were the warning buoys above a lengthy set of rapids. Lordy. Thankfully, the water was high, and the rapids were less of a factor.*
>
> *We quickly motored out of trouble's path.*
>
> *Our emotions jumped from concerned to frightened to relieved. A short time later, the sun burned through the fog, and we were back wearing sunglasses and acting like we knew what we were doing.*

Chapter 7 – Finally, Out on the Lake

Unfolding the map...
While on the subject of maps, it's a good place for this story. We were fishing about a mile from the above spot with two buoys. We were along the west shore of a long bay filled with islands – when we came upon a deep, narrow creek emptying into the bay. It was on the map – a clear position identifier.

Curious, we turned to journey up the creek, while examining the map to see where the creek originated – only to notice we'd gotten to the edge of our folded section. So, no problem, we just took the map from the Ziplock protector and unfolded it.

My first reaction was to be upset, as it appeared the map had somehow become wet and the printing ink had duplicated itself on another section. At the same time, our journey up the creek had taken us into a sizable burnt-out area – barren of trees due to a forest fire. It was moonlike and somewhat spooky.

As I looked more carefully at the map, I was shocked. As we knew, the lake consisted of two long parallel bodies of water (huge bays) covered with islands, with two passages between each, allowing transit from one to the other. Our fishing camp was at the end of one of those large bays.

What I first thought was an ink duplication...was actually two more huge bays parallel to the two we were familiar with. The narrow deepwater creek we'd discovered was the sole connection to another vast lake area.

Our boat drifted as we looked at the map and the two huge newly discovered bays, then at our barren, spooky, burnt-out surroundings. We remembered how we were already miles from camp and had not seen another boat for hours. We returned to the bays we were familiar with, which were a vast area on their own.

Get familiar with the boat & motor

When the camp operator issues you a boat and motor, it's best for all in your group to pay attention. How is the motor started? How is it put in gear, forward & reverse? How is it shut off? How is it raised partially or fully? How is the fuel tank connected and disconnected?

Operating an outboard is relatively easy. If no group member has recent experience, several of you should spend 30-40 mins operating it near the camp's boat dock. Practice starting and shutting off the motor (most are easily started). Practice putting it in forward and reverse. Practice turning – sharply; turn it with some speed crossing its wake. Operate it through turns while backing slowly – where most operating time will be spent. Make 5-6 practice approaches to the dock.

A routine question in boat safety courses…*"How fast do you approach a dock?"* The correct answer is *"No faster than you're willing to strike it."*

We don't clown around while out on the water. We move around very little in the boat while traveling at speed. We don't drink alcohol in the boat – it's illegal to drink alcohol while boating in Ontario.

 At every camp we've fished, we've been provided a sturdy, well-constructed 14 – 16' aluminum fishing boat – usually Lund's. The boats are equipped with modern 4-cycle outboards, usually 15-20hp. (We appreciate the 4-cycle engines, which are lubricated by oil in the crankcase – not mixed in the fuel.) They start easier, idle quieter, and don't give off oily smoke.

The 15-20hp motor with two or three in the boat, with our gear, is somewhat underpowered. We're sure the camp operators' strategy is that fishermen may bang into something, but they'll be doing it at a bit slower speed. We welcome that thinking – as it's less likely for us to get in trouble. Even then, many camps sell a 'damage coverage' should something happen to their boat or motor – we purchase it.

Even the Fly-in camps provide quality fishing boats. They fly the boats into their camps tied to the supports on the side of their float planes. It's something to see.

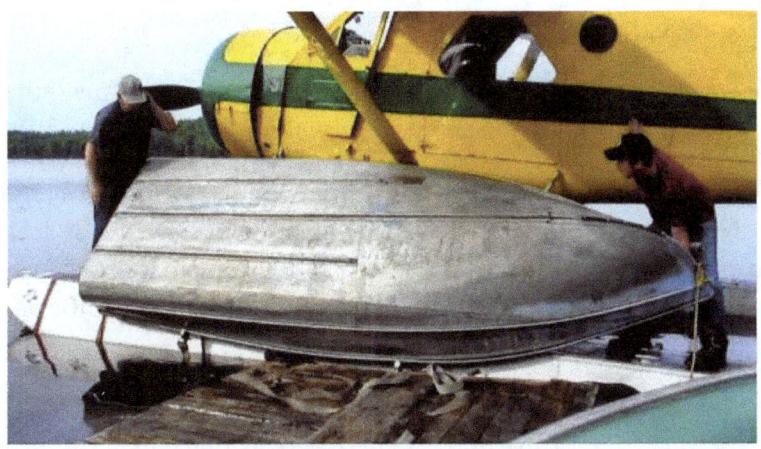

Being Prepared
Several years ago, my twin grandsons were approaching the age to operate my boat if they first took the state's boating safety course. It was online and free.

I thought, if I'm making them take the course, it's only right that I also take it (in this case, the Iowa Boating Safety Course).

Thinking I was an old hand at boating, having been boating for years, I told myself that when I get to the familiar sections, I'll just skip over those parts. Surprisingly, I never encountered the *'I know this stuff'* parts! There was so much I didn't know – and the course was so well prepared, with numerous videos. We'd recommend that each member of your group take this course.

Several in our group have taken boating safety and first aid courses.

In our watertight utility bag, we carry a first aid kit... a tarp that could serve as a crude shelter for an overnight stay, a length of rope, a roll of duct tape (to patch a hole in the hull, hopefully), and a flashlight.

(Remember, cell phones will likely have no service for most of these areas.)

We wear our auto-inflate lifejackets while moving at speed in the boat – and while fishing in rougher waters.

We stow and secure the gear in the boat when traveling at speed... so items won't vibrate onto the boat floor and under a seat or blow away in the breeze. We try to remember to bring minnow buckets and fish stringers back onboard. You'll remember after forgetting several times.

> *...without a paddle*
> *My good friend Dave and his guest were fishing a long Ontario lake-river system miles from my friend's cabin. It was late afternoon – about the time to call it quits and head in, when the outboard ran out of gas. My friend thought this was no problem, always having a spare fuel container on board.*
>
> *When Dave noticed the spare tank was missing, his guest confessed to having taken it out to make room for some of his gear.*
>
> *With one oar and a seat cushion, the two paddled through the night, past island after island, in what turned out to be the correct direction. They reached their destination as dawn arrived. It's no surprise, their friendship never seemed quite the same.*

Chapter 7 – Finally, Out on the Lake

Now that we've discussed the serious stuff, let's return to the fun items:

Finding fish

There are a gazillion books and YouTube videos sharing fishing techniques – we'll not duplicate those folks. Well, maybe just a couple of tips that might help.

As we return to a lake, each group member seems to have a favorite spot they'd like to fish. To cover those bases, we assign an area of the lake system for each day of our trip.

It allows us to cover favorite spots without undue transit time – as they can be miles apart.

New people in camp couldn't believe we'd leave a dynamite good area to fish elsewhere. Yes, and we don't look back.

As we shared, each morning, we tell the camp operator which area of their lake system we plan to fish in that day and ask him/her to suggest good spots there. (They know the waters better than anyone and want you to be successful.)

As a general rule, if the wind has been blowing in a particular direction for a few days, we'll head to the downwind side of the lake, where hopefully, the bait fish have been blown, followed by the game fish.

You're looking for a gravel and small pebble lake bottom for walleye.

We'll start fishing in a snaking path in varying distances from shore – over different water depths until we get bites. (Keeping an eye on the depth finder.) We'll then center on the depth where we find success.

It's the same with lures – each in our group starts with a different rig to see what might be working that day… (e.g., a minnow-tipped jib, a minnow-tipped spinner rig, a minnow-tipped Lindy Rig, etc.), and using different colors.

It may be helpful to share two fish-catching products that we wouldn't be without:

First is a bottom bouncer – a wire device that follows the lake bottom while trolling, helping to avoid being snagged on rocks. To catch walleye, it's important that you're on or near the bottom. The line to your rod is attached to the middle loop, and your hook on a 4-5ft of leader is fastened to the swivel end. While trolling, the weighted prong bounces off the bottom – and being just a wire, it avoids most snagging.

The second product is the Berkley scented bait **Gulp**, sold in various shapes and colors. In our opinion, it works as well as live minnows for about 20-30 minutes until its attractant odor is depleted.

We carry Gulp Recharge to refresh the attractant. It's a faint odor, but the fish recognize it – and that's what's important! We take various shapes, especially their swimming mullet shape in hot pink.

One lesson we stay mindful of is barometric pressure and its effect on fishing success. Pressure below 29.6 usually results in poor fishing; pressures between 29.8 and 30.2 produce more success. We can't change it, but it helps to explain the fish activity – or lack of.

We know of a particular bay where walleye are difficult on sunny, calm water days – but bring in some clouds and breeze, with light waves, and get out the dip net. (That's why they call it a *'walleye chop.'*)

There are a gazillion fishing videos on TV and YouTube. We'd suggest starting with those featuring Al Lindner or Gary Roach; their lessons are excellent.

Using Guides
If you're new to fishing or new to the lake area (or even if you're experienced), we'd highly suggest hiring a fishing guide early in the trip. Besides finding fish, there is no end to the suggestions and lessons you'll learn, plus just having a fun time… all for the per-day fee.

We think back to many of the little skills and habits our group takes for granted today, that came from the time we spent with an experienced guide.

For example, we learned some of the science behind finding fish, the baits and tackle for specific situations, proper boat operation while trolling, and dozens of other tips. Plus, it's just fun meeting someone with such skills and hearing their stories.

Many Northwoods guides include fixing shore lunches in their fee.

Guides cost about $250-$300 per day; he or she will join you in your boat or theirs; some have half-day rates. Usually, a 15-20% gratuity is shared. We've never regretted the cost!

A note of caution: Don't be a stinker and follow a guide who's out with another group. Pass the hat and hire the guide for your group. The guides need to make a living. There's much more to gain than learning a few of his/her fishing spots.

Fishing limits
Your camp operator will share the rules and limits for the species you're after. They're eager for you to have fishing success while conserving the resources for future seasons.

Some camps have done such an excellent job in fish stewardship with their lakes – that they're seeing fish numbers and sizes increasing yearly.

We are ardent fish conservationists – we understand they're a precious resource. (I suppose if we were really serious, we'd throw them all back, ha… that's not going to happen.) We keep only two per day per person (per the Ontario Conservation license), remaining within the size rules and throwing the larger ones back. It makes sense.

> *Northern pike for lunch…*
> *We usually take filleted walleye in a Ziplock on ice out with us in the morning for that day's shore lunch. But one day, we didn't have any fillets but told ourselves we had all morning to catch our shore lunch.*
>
> *During the morning, as luck would have it… We were struggling to get a walleye to bite. (Yes, even in Canada, this can happen for a period of time.) We'd picked an unfortunate morning for it to happen to us – (no way would our pride have allowed us to bring sandwiches.)*

Chapter 7 – Finally, Out on the Lake

Our fellow operating the outboard and seeking favorable spots was frustrated – and said, 'Well, what are we going to do?'

One in our group then said, 'Let's try this...' holding up a favorite northern pike lure.

We all quickly rigged up for northern fishing and viola – we soon had two nice ones for the frying pan – delicious!

A quiet moment
We were two fishermen each in two boats, and decided to drift fish down a short (¼ mile) stream that connected two bodies of water. The gentle current was perfect for drift fishing; I used a minnow-tipped jig.

The two boats became separated, with one starting the ¼ mile drift as the other reached the far end.

We were concentrating on our fishing and where the drift was taking us as we turned to head back to the upper current end.

There, standing in the water between our two boats, was a full-size female moose!

Both boats shut their motors off and enjoyed the moment...I have always wished I'd had a camera. (This image is close to what we experienced that day.)

CHAPTER 8

Fixing Shore Lunch

Shore lunches began when early fishing guides, needing to feed their fishermen of the day, would clean and fry up some of the morning's catch over a fire. Simply preparing a meal grew to include delicious fish breading, batters, and side dishes – as a guide's cooking reputation added to their fish-finding skills.

Yes, without a guide, shore lunches are not as simple as eating a sandwich, and having the gear in the boat is somewhat bothersome – but these lunches have provided us with such memories and good food that we couldn't picture ourselves not doing it.

Sitting on a rock, viewing the lake scenery, and enjoying freshly fried walleye – we laugh and agree that the old-timers knew what they were doing. Our sons and grandsons think shore lunches are the highlight of our trips.

Tell your camp operator the day before when you'd like to have a shore lunch (we do this every day). In the morning, the camp will have a Rubbermaid chest and LP burner sitting on the dock, ready to be placed in your boat.

In the camp's shore lunch chest, you'll find dishes and utensils, a cast iron fry pan, a cooking pot, a spatula, a can or two of vegetables, usually some bread and butter, several cookies, a can opener, matches, salt and pepper, paper towels, and a trash bag for debris. We use most of their items and add a few of our own:

- We bring our non-stick fry pan and a quality spatula.

- Our fish breading (in a Ziplock bag), cooking oil, and our fillets on ice.

- Our vegetables (we especially like the season's fresh asparagus).

- A long-nose fire lighter, quality oven mitts.

- And bug spray.

Ask your camp operator to recommend shore lunch spots in the part of the lake you're heading. You're looking for a somewhat level place, easy to beach or tie up the boat, and maybe with a previously established plank or rock ledge – so you're not cooking on the ground. (We don't take a folding table, but as we get older, it's a thought.)

Our first step at the lunch site is to stand upwind and spray bug repellent – allowing it to drift over the shore lunch area before food preparations. Surprisingly, we've seldom had a serious mosquito problem during our lunches. A little breeze helps.

Preparing shore lunch
If you aren't bringing fillets, someone in your group can fillet some of your morning catch on a flat rock, rinsing them in the lake. (We prefer to bring iced fillets caught the afternoon before – allowing us to use the camp's fish cleaning shack.)

With only one burner, the cook now needs a little magic. We'll first heat the side dish(es) in a pot, like the potatoes, sweet corn, asparagus, or baked beans – put the lid on, and set it aside while heating the oil and frying the walleye. When the walleye is done, reheating the side dish(es) takes just a moment.

If you're having fried potatoes, we like to parboil them in the cabin until about half done – to speed up the shore lunch cooking. We'll also chop up onions in the cabin and take them in a plastic bag – to simplify things out on the island. A separate pan for each side dish – makes it easier to heat them. Hopefully, you can get each to share a portion of the burner top.

Coleman's portable 2-burner stove – perfect for shore lunches

Now, let's heat the oil to fry the walleye. We often use canola oil, which has a neutral flavor and is tolerant of a high temperature. I also like olive oil. You know the oil is the right temperature when a little dab of flour fizzles away quickly or a small piece of bread turns brown.

Place your fillets in the Ziplock bag with flour/breading and shake to coat each. (Do not reuse any of the bags after holding the walleye.)

We prefer plain flour for our breading. We don't eat walleye often enough to experiment with seasoned variations – salt and pepper are all the seasoning we need.

Now, place the filets in the hot oil with the outer surface down (to prevent their curling). You're looking for a golden-brown color. Turn just once if you can. Using a spatula and fork helps prevent the filets from breaking apart when turned.

Have the plates and utensils laid out – and warn the others that lunch is nearly ready.

Once the walleye is done, place the fillets on paper towels to absorb oil. Place the side dish pan(s) back on the burner; they'll reheat quickly. In a moment, you'll all be eating.

After several fried walleye lunches, we find preparing cheeseburgers or chili dogs to be a welcome change. Just remember the buns and mustard.

Chapter 8 – Fixing Shore Lunch

We take an 8'x10' poly tarp and a length of rope (stored in our utility bag) to fix over the burner when it's raining. You don't want to be near hot oil when raindrops are falling. On other occasions, the tarp shields the fire from the wind.

And speaking of wind, we don't care to cook over a bonfire. A portable LP burner makes shore lunches easier and quicker. Just set the burner in place, light it – and you'll be heating side dishes and frying fish in minutes. Turn off the burner, let it cool a few minutes, and voilá, you're back fishing – with no smoke blowing in your eyes or soot blackening the pots.

After eating, we rinse the plates, utensils, and pans in the lake. The cold lake water doesn't clean oily surfaces well, but we do as well as we can – paper towels are helpful. You just want pans and plates clean enough, not to mess up the shore lunch tote. The paper and other debris go in a trash bag; plates, utensils, and pans go in the camp's shore lunch box. And once the propane burner cools, we and the gear are back in the boat, (yes, it fits).

Back in camp, we remove our items and take the shore lunch box to the lodge, where their items are washed and readied for the next day. We wash our items.

This 14-minute video shares the steps of a professional fishing guide to prepare his shore lunches. It's well done.

'Shore lunch with Anderson's Lodge'
https://www.youtube.com/watch?v=NUEdfiiyYbc

'Coal to Newcastle'
My dear friend Matt called his Canadian fishing guide/outfitter to see if everything was ready for their arrival in several days. (Always a good idea!) On this occasion, the guide (an

The Canadian Fishing Adventure

Indigenous person) asked my friend to bring several cans of wild rice for their shore lunches.

With some difficulty, my friend found canned wild rice, which the guide later combined with fried potatoes to make a delicious side dish with their walleye. (It does sound good!)

Well, what made us laugh is how wild rice is usually harvested exclusively by 'native Americans and Canadians – making the bringing of store-bought wild rice for an Indigenous prepared shore lunch – like bringing 'coal to Newcastle.'

CHAPTER

Heading Home

Sadly, our fun time in the woods must come to an end. I enjoy the excitement of catching fish, seeing wildlife – like eagles and moose, and hanging with the guys, but when the time comes, I'm usually ready to head home (but not necessarily welcoming the return to work.)

On the last afternoon in camp, usually before supper, we pour ourselves a drink and start removing the reels, disassembling the rods, and preparing other gear for travel. We take a shower and change into our travel clothes, packing the dirty items and, again, leaving the rain gear on top.

If we are Fly-in or Boat-in, our group leader visits with the camp operator, sharing our desire to be on the first plane or boat leaving in the morning.

If we had to prepare dinner that evening, afterward, we would box up our kitchen gear and unused grocery items, liquor, snacks, etc., dividing it among the group or leaving it for the camp operator. We pride ourselves on leaving our cabins cleaner than when we arrived.

Take the note paper you brought and make a checklist for the morning, listing items to remember in the hectic departure. On top of the list is getting your frozen fish from the freezer and packing it for travel. We suggest keeping them all together in one cooler for now.

Paying the bill
Usually, after the last evening meal, the camp operators come to your cabin with bills for each occupant. They will expect payment at that time. Hopefully, they shared the form of payment requested in advance (or you remembered to ask). One camp we frequent requires a US bank cashier's check, which is fine – one just needs to be prepared.

They will have itemized the fee for the days spent and the incidentals, such as float plane service, meals eaten, beverages and bait purchased, etc.

At this point, each group member adds an amount to their payment as a gratuity to be shared with the camp's staff – like the lodge cook, waitresses, and dock workers who've provided bait, cleaned the boat each morning, or stored your frozen fish.

Rather than a percentage, I usually add a round amount to my lodging payment (like $100-150) to be shared among the staff. If an individual were extra helpful, I'd personally slip them another one or two US $20 bills (remember, you and they may be returning).

For fishing guides with whom we have spent the day and enjoyed, our group will quickly huddle after the day and either add ~20% to our payment for the day or each share $20-30 cash.

The float plane service is often incorporated into the fly-in lodge's fee. You may also have different pilots flying you in and out. Therefore, we again get our heads together and each share $10-$15 at the end of each flight.

CHAPTER 9 – HEADING HOME

If you're paying the lodging fee for an accompanying family member, remember to include a bit of gratuity for them.

Keeping some $5 and $10 bills at hand is helpful for incidental gratuity purposes. When a staff member brings a forgotten tackle box to your cabin – slipping them a $5 bill is appreciated.

Early departure
The morning when you depart, if you're on the first plane or boat out of camp, you'll need to have the gear and yourselves ready early. We skip breakfast – and plan to have something at a drive-up in one of the towns we'll pass through.

Like when you arrive, the camp operators will help get gear from the cabin to the dock and loaded on the plane or launch. Again, check that your gear is well labeled and counted to prevent confusion.

Due to mosquitos, we continue wearing slacks and something with long sleeves until we reach the vehicle – and if we choose, we change to more comfortable travel clothing for the trip back home. (Yes, in the parking lot, again, you won't be the first.)

If you're at a Fly-in or Boat-in location and it's raining, you'll want to wear your rain gear – at least the jacket. A supply of trash bags will come in handy to protect gear from the rain.

We'd arrived and departed from Boat-in camps numerous times, always in ideal weather…enjoying the scenery and someone else driving. We'd ask each other what this journey would be like in the rain.

Well, one morning, we and another group were the first to jointly leave camp – a stiff cold wind with rain was pounding the cabin.

We had a schedule, and new guests would be arriving. If we'd been flying, no one would have been moving, but while it wasn't pleasant, the launches could travel.

We quickly double-bagged luggage and gear with trash bags so that rain would not harm them. Thankfully, we had plenty of trash bags. I placed my laptop in a large Ziplock bag, then inside its carrying bag...then double-bagged it in trash bags and carried it myself during the transit.

The launch ride was an experience. The boat operator sat behind a small windshield and wore goggles to help see as we sped through the driving rain. Those of us riding faced the rear – we'd briefly turn to look forward only to have our faces blasted with rain.

After finally arriving at the landing near the parking lot, we quickly backed our vehicles down and loaded the baggage – hoping we got our gear in the correct vehicles. Off we went – now fully aware of what the Boat-in transit was like in the rain.

After getting home, we laid everything out in the sun to dry – all the gear, including the laptop, was fine.

Fish inspections

You may think this is a strange place to discuss this topic – let us explain.

In northwest Ontario, only two or three roads lead in and out of the lake areas. Most fisherman leave their camps on Friday or Saturday, and almost all travel these two or three roads on those mornings.

With this natural funneling of visiting fishermen, the Ontario game wardens find it easier to set up checkpoints at pull-off areas

Chapter 9 – Heading Home

along those routes.

Game wardens can appear at fishing camps, checking freezers and refrigerators – or drop in by float plane to check fishermen's stringers on the lake, but there's a reason the only time we've been checked over the many years, is the morning roadside stops – it's just more efficient for the officials. These checks occur outside communities on logging truck pull-offs, miles north of the border – for us, it seems to occur on about 1 out of 4-5 trips.

The vehicles with US plates are waved over, and occupants are asked to get out and have their fish and fishing licenses ready for review.

The game warden will carefully examine each person's fishing license and packaged frozen fish – hopefully, packaged per their rules:

No more than two filets frozen, laying flat, and clearly visible in a Zip-lock bag, with enough skin left attached to identify the species. (The two filets don't have to be from the same fish, for those trying to share meat quantity equally among the group.)

In our group, some individuals don't care to take northern pike home, while others are eager to have them. (Northern is good to eat and usually provides more meat than walleye.) We'll freeze a maximum of two northern pike per person (per the Ontario Conservation license). But we don't label them all as belonging to the recipient, or place them all in that person's cooler. You don't want to give a game warden cause to believe the larger count was caught by one individual.

Be careful when game wardens ask questions!
The game warden knows that it takes time for fillets to freeze hard. Since fish in the freezer count as being 'in your possession',

have your group members use caution if asked, *'Did you enjoy walleye for supper last night?'* The official is not just chatting.

Your answer needs to be *'We ate in the lodge,'* or something other than your having eaten walleye.

Sorry, yes, the game wardens can be devious.

Border crossing
Just before we reach the US border, we have another opportunity to purchase duty-free goods, such as tobacco, liquor, etc. We take advantage of this, as the price for top-labeled liquors is inviting.

But a word of caution: Canadian duty-free stores often sell Cuban cigars; these are not permitted entry into the US.

A short distance later, you're at the US border station. All the suggestions we shared when approaching the Canadian border station also apply here – all in the vehicle should have their passports in hand, be alert, remove their sunglasses, and lower all the driver's side windows. Again, this is no time for clowning around.

They will check each passport. Again, there are a gazillion cameras on you and the vehicle. You'll be asked where you've been, how long you were in Canada, the purpose of your trip, where you're going, etc.

Once you say you've been fishing, they ask how many fish you have with you. We politely answer them, but we always wondered why they cared. We didn't catch them in the US. I understand they have general concerns over poaching and smuggling. And we realize their questions are as much to see our reactions and how we frame the response.

Chapter 9 – Heading Home

Once we've passed the US border station, we quickly fill up with cheaper US gasoline (less tax) and divide up our frozen fish as desired – before making our way home.

The ride home is an opportunity to note additions to our packing checklist and improvements to the menu or lodging arrangements (and who to re-invite next year)

THE CANADIAN FISHING ADVENTURE

CHAPTER

You'll want to avoid these…

Avoid following other boats – or fishing close to others
Fishermen are attracted to the lakes we describe – because they have fish and fewer people. And, it's relaxing. When you're enjoying yourselves in a small bay…the last thing you want, with miles of shoreline to fish, is another boat to pull in close by.

Be a good sportsman and fish elsewhere for a bit…the other boat will move along, and then you can try that spot.

Take a guide along on one of the first days of your trip. It can be so helpful – you will fish the guide's favorite spots and learn what makes those spots successful, and how to identify similar sites yourself.

Avoid striking a moose
Driving through the Northwoods is picturesque, with miles of forest and lakes. It's pristine, with stretches of few dwellings or businesses or even traffic. But after a bit, a driver can become drowsy. You're not paying attention – and suddenly, a giant moose is on the road right before you.

They're huge, more the size of a horse than a deer. The threat is the massive animal sliding over your vehicle's hood, smashing through the windshield and then crashing into the passenger compartment.

Your best defense is to:

1. Avoid driving in the dark

2 Avoid high speeds – leave yourself reaction time; and

3. The driver should remain alert – visit with passengers, open a window, get out and walk around the car, or take a nap.

Don't clown around during the border crossings
Heading north, you're in a jovial mood – heading for your long-awaited fishing adventure. In the process, some of those in the vehicle may be tempted to crack jokes or make glib comments while being questioned by the Canadian border officer.

As we have shared, border entry points are one of few places (in Canada or the US) where officials need no warrant or probable cause to search your vehicle and luggage.

Chapter 10 – You'll Want to Avoid These

We do everything we can think of to not give the officers reason to delay us. We have the inside of our vehicle straightened up and looking tidy; everyone is sitting up erect in their seats, no one is wearing sunglasses. Both passenger-side windows are rolled down. Our passports are in hand. We're prepared for an 'all-business' serious conversation. If all goes well, in 2-3 minutes, you're on your way.

Avoid 'No-See-Um' insects
The warm months in the Northwoods produce mosquitoes. We wear a light application of a repellent with the active ingredient DEET; it helps. We'll wear slacks and long sleeves for protection and stay indoors or on the lake.

We encountered one camp where we were introduced to No-See-Ums, an insect so tiny they pass through window screens. I can say I have never seen one – but have been bitten without mercy.

The bite lasts longer than a mosquito bite and itches more.

My first suggestion is to avoid locations with No-See-Ums. To us, they don't seem to be everywhere, like mosquitos. We've been to camps where we've never had a No-See-Um bite – and others where it was a real problem.

It's so frustrating, you (I) never see the insect, and you don't know there's a problem until after you've been bitten. Most of our bites were received in our cabin – we didn't realize the window screens didn't stop them.

We would apply DEET, even to sleep, with little effect. We now understand repellents with picaridin and permethrin outperform DEET for No-See-Ums. Surprisingly, Avon Skin So Soft lotion, long known for its insect-repelling abilities, is 10% picaridin.

If I HAD to spend time in a camp with No-See-Ums knowingly, I'd take a picaridin repellent and sleep under a fine-mesh bed screen designed to repel No-See-Ums.

Without question, these chemicals are unhealthy (we just hope the repellent is slightly better than bug bites). We use the least amount possible and for as little time as possible.

My cousin points out... that the camp operators themselves don't seem as bothered by insects – and without using repellent. We've also noticed this and we're not sure exactly why. What we do know is – the insects are attracted to us.

Avoid over drinking
All in our group enjoy an adult beverage – or two. One of the leading reasons for such an outing is to have a beverage with buddies, put your feet up, laugh, and visit. While drinking is enjoyable, we can't count the situations marred by someone's over-drinking.

The group dynamics are stressful enough – being close for several days without adding extra drama. As we get older, we drink less and get to bed sooner. It sure helps our performance the next day. We're reminded that Ontario has made drinking alcohol in boats illegal.

Besides limiting our drinking, we avoid conflict activities like discussing politics, serious betting, and encouraging each other's private time – all to help us better enjoy our days together.

Avoid being injured by fish hooks.
You'll be spending hours fishing – and that will have you tying on lures and jigs with hooks, casting lures with hooks, baiting hooks, and hopefully, unhooking fish. We recognize the danger

Chapter 10 – You'll Want to Avoid These

of sharp hooks and treat them with the same caution as a sharp knife. (To add insult, we frequently re-sharpen our hooks to ensure they perform well.)

We use extra caution with each cast to keep the lure away from ourselves and others, especially when it's windy. If there's any doubt, wait to cast until there's room to do it more carefully.

When tying on hooks and lures, loosen the line so it's not under tension. Hold the hook by the bottom curved part rather than the shank. (If the line should be jerked, the hook will pull harmlessly from your fingers.)

When removing a hook from a fish flopping on the boat floor, release the line tension and lay the rod down. Use long-nose pliers or a hemostat to grasp the hook, twisting it to release it from the fish's mouth. If you must hold the fish, with a glove on your less dominant hand, hold the fish's body (either against the boat's floor or grasped firmly around its body). Using your dominant hand, grasp and twist the hook with the hemostat.

Once the hook or lure is free from the fish (while still attached to the line), toss it over the edge of the boat into the water, ensuring it stays clear of people as you give high-fives, take pictures, string up the fish, and rearrange yourself. Avoid letting lures/hooks flop loosely from upright rods – secure the hook to a rod guide and tighten the line.

When a fighting fish puts tension on the line, and the rod is bent, try not to allow the tension to be in line with harming yourself or others. The fish may release the lure/hook, and it will come flying back. Holding the rod tip down or toward the front or back of the boat minimizes this threat.

Some fishermen use barbless hooks to reduce the danger. Wearing eyewear is also best.

Avoiding being the rude American

As Americans, we're proud of our country; that's good, we should be. I've lived in different countries – guess what, they were also proud of THEIR country. That's true of Canadians. They don't view themselves as living in the northern suburbs of America.

Please treat them with the respect you'd like for yourself. Avoid the jokes and off-color humor. You'll be more welcome – as will those of us who follow you.

Avoid bringing Handguns; they're not welcome

Handguns are not allowed unless you have the proper registration certificate. Concealed carry is prohibited – except for specific occupations. Rifles and shotguns intended for hunting are more welcome with the proper paperwork.

Personal defense pepper spray is prohibited, but its cousin, bear spray, is allowed. The label must declare that its intended use is for animals…and approved by the United States Environmental Protection Agency (USEPA), which must be on the label. Carrying bear spray in non-wildlife areas puts you back in the illegal status.

Surprisingly, Byrna defensive air pistols are legal in Canada (the Canadian government carved out a special allowance in their law, permitting the Byrna air weapon.)

Radar detectors are legal in the far western provinces – Saskatchewan, Alberta, and British Columbia – but not in other provinces. CB radios are allowed in all of Canada.

CHAPTER

Emergencies

Emergencies are better handled when there's a plan in place and the plans are better developed with a cool head – before the screaming and drama sets in.

Let's look at several situations:

A serious injury or health issue
In our Northwoods activities, we avoid taking dangerous risks, because we're miles from help – but still, things can happen... severe cuts (while cleaning a fish), burns (when lighting a fire), wounds (from fish hooks), broken bones (from a fall), etc. For this reason, it would be very helpful if one or two of your group had basic first aid training.

We like the military version of the First Aid **ABC**'s:
   Clear the **A**irway – return breathing
   Stop the **B**leeding -pressure bandage/tourniquet
   Control shock, incline their feet

Camp operators are our first resource for help, so return to camp as quickly as possible. They will have more first-aid supplies and the ability to communicate with medical personnel. They can call in a float plane for transport to a hospital. We doubt if you'll have a problem they haven't seen.

Existing medical issues

We would guess that a greater percentage of those traveling north to fish are older, retired, and are men, many with some form of ailment – especially coronary issues.

It would be wise for those with known conditions to visit with their physician and the camp operator well before departing home. Share your ailment and the likelihood of a problem re-occurring – and the likely treatment you'll need if that should happen. They will help determine whether the fishing camp is the place for you or how best they'll deal with a situation should you need help.

We've fished from camps that were 30 minutes by car from the nearest hospital and some that were an hour by float plane from medical care – and that's after the plane arrived.

Those using CPAP machines will want to discuss this with the camp operator. Again, you won't be the first. Is your machine's electrical needs compatible with the camp's generator? Will your machine's battery continue operating late at night when the camp's generator is shut down?

Problem with insurance coverage

Unfortunately, most US health insurers, including Medicare, do not extend their coverage to Canada.

Contact your health insurance provider to include temporary Canadian medical services – or purchase stand-alone international medical coverage for your trip.

Problems back home

What if a calamity occurs back home – or at your workplace, while you're up north?

Chapter 11 – Emergencies

All the outlying camps we've fished from had some form of two-way communication, usually a satellite telephone. Ask the camp operator for their camp phone number. Note: This may be a different number than what is shared in their advertising.

When you need to leave quickly
What would you do if something serious happened back home and you needed to return quickly? Would your group have to discontinue their having fun and take you home?

If the need arose, and money was an issue, possibly someone in your group could drive you halfway south while someone, like a spouse, at the same time drove halfway north. You meet up for your continued journey home. It would cost your friend in the group a day of fishing – but you might think of a way to make it up.

If money were less of an issue, there would be more options. Surprisingly, many of the towns in the Northwoods have taxi services, and some have multiple taxis. They could pick you up at the float plane dock, boat-in landing…or your drive-in camp… and transport you to the nearest airport with scheduled flights. Viola, you're on your way.

Some communities have familiar rental car outlets (Enterprise, National…), where they say you can rent a one-way vehicle to a sister rental outlet near your home in the States. Their willingness to rent one-way may depend upon vehicle availability. You can picture the situation – at least, it's a possibility.

If money is not an issue, you can arrange a charter flight using an aircraft from near your home or vice versa using an aircraft from a nearby Canadian airport. Just take a short car ride to any nearby Canadian airfield, load your stuff in the aircraft, and

The Canadian Fishing Adventure

you're en route to your hometown airport – with a short visit along the way with US Customs.

– Epilogue –

"Many men go fishing all of their lives without knowing that it is not fish they are after."

– Henry David Thoreau

Having reached an age when a person's health starts closing in on future Northwoods adventures – we fondly look back at our many pre-dawn departures headed northward – the air filled with excitement. We remember the humorous and embarrassing incidents – like fixing omelets for breakfast with dreadful sharp cheddar cheese…or forgetting to replace the boat's drain plug. And, of course, the endless stories told after someone said, 'Do you remember…?'

And with that – forgive me for sharing one last story I just remembered.

We were fishing on one of Ontario's 'portage-in' lakes. Our camp operator kept a boat and motor on the lake – we just needed to carry in basic fishing gear and a gas can. It was now late afternoon – we'd had another great day fishing.

I was running the motor, and the other two fellows were dozing. We were headed back to the portage way and then an hour-plus boat ride back to camp.

I was running at speed up a half-mile-long, 200-foot-wide lake slot cut through the forest. The sound of the motor was also making me dozy.

Then, SWOOSH a giant shadow silently came from behind, just a few feet above me. By instinct, I ducked down – thinking it was a float plane gliding in. When I regained my breath, I recognized

The Canadian Fishing Adventure

a huge eagle gliding out ahead and slightly above us – wings extending at least as wide as our boat.

It continued gliding straight ahead and finally started climbing back over the forest…I'm sure it was anxious to tell its mate how it had shown the silly fishermen whose lake it was.

Glossary

Beaver – a heavy-hauling Canadian-produced float plane. Its rugged build and powerful radial engine make it popular for civilian, government, and military uses.

Boat-in – a camp whose guests arrive by boat

Camp operator – the person(s) in charge of the fishing camp – often a husband-wife team

Drive-in camp – a camp whose guests arrive in their vehicle

Eh – a brief slang term inferring agreement to the statement

Fishing Camp – We use the terms *camp, fishing camp, lodge, and resort* interchangeably. This is a Northwoods business that supplies lodging, boats, and possibly meals, in our case mainly for visiting fishermen and hunters.

Fly-in camp – a camp whose guests must arrive by float plane.

Jigs/jigging – fish hooks with a small lead weight used by jerking the line up and down off the lake bottom. They are often painted and have a plastic skirt, feathers, tinsel, etc. and can be used with a minnow, nightcrawler or leech.

Lindy Rigs – a sinker allowed to slide on the line, stopped by a swivel to which a leader and hook are attached. The sinker keeps the hook down and trailing behind – when a fish bites, the line slides through the sinker to not alarm the fish.

Marabou jig – a painted lead head jig with Marabou (turkey) feathers tied around the hook's shank.

Noorduyn Norseman – a brute of a single-engine float plane produced in Canada for backcountry and military uses. Its successor was the Beaver.

Northwoods – we're referring to the large areas of forested land covering much of Canada, including northern parts of Minnesota, Wisconsin, and Michigan. (A large portion is defined as a 'boreal forest' – primarily evergreen, extending far north and transitioning into tundra.)

Outfitter – a firm providing some or all needs for outdoorsmen… supplies, guiding, lodging, meals and/or transportation.

Out-post cabin – an outlying, remote cabin whose occupants arrive by float plane or boat.

Shore lunch – most often a fried fish meal prepared in rustic style along the shore.

Spinner Rigs – a fishing lure formed with a hook usually separated by colorful beads from a shiny metal spinner; often used when trolling.

Walleye chop – small wavelets caused by a 10-15mph breeze.

Contributors

We thank these outstanding individuals and dear friends for their contributions in making this book possible, all are avid Canadian fishermen:

Scott Tatman – My youngest son and avid hunter and fisherman lives outside Los Angeles – he takes the red-eye flight from LA to Minneapolis, where we commencer our drive into northern Ontario. His older brother, Tony, declines our invitations, but we don't give up.

Terry Lininger – The author's cousin, who, much like his father George, would rather be fishing than doing almost anything else.

Darrell Witte, a retired co-worker and one of our fishing group – sometimes joined by his son Matt. Darrell and the author enjoy outings in Canada, Minnesota, and Arizona.

Mike Phelps is a retired co-worker and hunter-fisherman whose background mirrors the author's; while working, the two Mikes traveled together through dozens of states. They believe they called on more ag-businesses than any other two in the US.

Wayne Ellertson is a retired co-worker and long-time chum and the one who originated the author's fishing group – often joined by his grandson, **Kevin Amos**, who was always welcome.

Dave Carpenter – a dear Lake Okoboji friend who has fished Ontario for years – from his own Northwoods property.

Matt Bauer, another treasured friend from Lake Okoboji, who routinely takes his grandsons on fishing outings to Canada - when he's not farming.

Larry Braby, a dear Lake Okoboji chum who loves hunting and fishing, especially in Canada, and then – writing about his outdoor adventures, Larry's first book, *'You Had To Be There.'*

Sanford Reed is a much-missed deceased neighbor who, along with his wife, loved fishing in Canada and elsewhere. Besides being a neighbor, Sanford was a friend!

Don Luetkeman, sadly, another deceased neighbor and great fellow, who was able to fit farming into his fishing. We're sure the border officials called him 'Don.'

Larry Halverson is a retired co-worker and one of our original fishing group – a fellow Vietnam veteran and treasured friend.

Acknowledgments

The author gratefully appreciates **Mr. Ryan Runge** and his Slate Falls Outposts for allowing the use of the cover image. Mr. Runge can be reached at **SlateFallsOutposts.com.**

We thank the very skilled and patient **Debbie Wilson** and **Lisa Graham Peterson** for providing the author with valuable technical assistance in preparing this writing.

About the author

M.C. 'Mike' Tatman grew up on the grounds of a rural grain business. Surrounded by commodity-hauling trucks, rail cars, and storage and production facilities, it was exciting for a young boy.

After graduating from Minnesota State University and serving three tours in Vietnam, he began a career insuring ag businesses. Here, he and several co-workers spent vacations fishing in the Northwoods.

Their over 40 years of fishing trips encompassed dozens of Canadian drive-in, boat-in, and fly-in destinations. From young men themselves, the group has grown to include sons and grandsons – all having fond memories of past trips – and anxious for their next Northwoods outing.

This writing follows Mike's first published book, *'Reduce the Mayhem - Discover More Profits,'* directed towards corporate management.

Available on Amazon

Our Northwoods ✓ Packing Checklist

Traveling to and from your Destination (ideally in a smaller duffle)

- ☐ 2-3 pairs of underwear
- ☐ 1-2 pairs of socks
- ☐ 2-3 golf polo shirts
- ☐ 1 – handkerchief
- ☐ One sweater, sweatshirt or light jacket
- ☐ Wearing either cargo shorts or slacks, and packing the other (for travel & the lodge)
- ☐ Wearing comfortable travel shoes for the vehicle, and worn in the camp

Toiletries kit, including:

- ☐ Toothpaste & brush
- ☐ Shaver
- ☐ Deodorant
- ☐ Prescription Medicines
- ☐ 5-6 loose Band-Aids
- ☐ Fingernail clipper
- ☐ Hand/skin lotion
- ☐ Aleve or Advil (for pain)
- ☐ Aleve PM or Tylenol PM (sleep aid)
- ☐ Neosporin cream (for pains, antiseptic, burns)
- ☐ Bactine 1st aid spray (relieves pain & itching, cuts, scrapes, burns)

The Canadian Fishing Adventure

- ☐ Kaopectate chews (anti-diarrhea)
- ☐ Milk of Magnesia chews (for constipation)
- ☐ Zicam, under tongue lozenge (take at the first sign of cold)
- ☐ Chloraseptic throat spray
- ☐ Alka-Seltzer Plus or Coricidin (for colds)
- ☐ Zyrtec – (for allergies -the forest is full of pollens)

Miscellaneous: (either on our person or in the small duffle)

- ☐ Billfold (Driver's license, credit cards, health insurance card and $cash)
- ☐ Cell phone – and charger
- ☐ Passport (When not traveling, I keep this in the bottom of my toiletries kit, in a plastic Ziplock w/ some emergency cash; when not in Canada, I keep the fishing license and Outdoor Card in this same bag)
- ☐ Sunglasses, and retaining strap (Ideally polarized – which allows seeing below the water surface, important when dip-netting a fighting fish.)
- ☐ Map/directions to the destination & the camp's phone number
- ☐ Payment for fishing camp (cashier's check, credit card, cash ... consider a gratuity for workers)
- ☐ Auto insurance card and vehicle registration (kept in the vehicle glovebox)
- ☐ Flashlight – with fresh batteries
- ☐ Spare eyeglasses
- ☐ Spare car keys
- ☐ Medical bracelet
- ☐ This book

Packing for camp & fishing: (in hard totes or larger duffles)

- ☐ 4-5 pairs of underwear

- ☐ 4-5 short-sleeve & 2 long-sleeve T-shirts
- ☐ 4-5 short-sleeve & 2 long-sleeve polo tops
- ☐ Socks for each day
- ☐ 2- bath towels
- ☐ Pillow (The utility bag is a good place to pack your pillow for boat-in & fly-in transits)
- ☐ Ear muffs (to silence snoring)
- ☐ Hand soap & shampoo
- ☐ Paper towels (2-3 rolls if you're cooking)
- ☐ Trash bags (a box of 20 heavy-duty garbage can size)
- ☐ Plastic drinking glasses (desired size for cocktails)
- ☐ Kleenex
- ☐ 4 x 6" notepad and pen
- ☐ Sharpie pen
- ☐ Bug spray
- ☐ Bottled water
- ☐ Two extension cords with multi-plug-in connectors
- ☐ Small electric fan (optional)
- ☐ 11-watt LED bulb. (optional)
- ☐ One small Igloo cooler per person (for iced fillets & beverages for the boat; and taking frozen fish home)

Apparel for Fishing:
- ☐ Cold weather sweater
- ☐ 2- pair fishing slacks
- ☐ Hooded sweatshirt

The Canadian Fishing Adventure

☐ Rain suit (packed on top of travel chest)

☐ Outdoor footwear

☐ Rubber boots (optional)

☐ Gloves

☐ Brimmed Hat

☐ Stocking cap

☐ Light down jacket/vest (optional)

Kitchen items (if you're cooking)

☐ 1-quality utility knife

☐ 1-quality metal spatula

☐ 1-Pair quality kitchen hot mitts.

☐ 1-full size non-stick fry pan

☐ 2-3 rolls of paper towels

☐ Several dishwashing rags & drying towels

☐ Daily planned menu – and recipes

☐ Salt & pepper

☐ One box, (30) 1-gal Ziplock freezer bags

☐ One Ziplock bag with ½ cup flour in each – for each day of planned shore lunches.

☐ Coffee percolator – optional

Grocery items (based on menu choices)

Non-perishable items purchased in the US, like…

☐ Canned vegetables, soups, stews…

☐ Condiment packets

The Canadian Fishing Adventure

- ☐ Cooking oil
- ☐ Salt & pepper
- ☐ Dish soap
- ☐ Pan scrubber
- ☐ Bottled water – soft drinks
- ☐ Snacks
- ☐ Coffee & filters

Perishable groceries purchased in Canada, like…

- ☐ Bread
- ☐ Butter
- ☐ Milk
- ☐ Sliced cheese -for omelets, cheeseburgers, grilled cheese
- ☐ Eggs
- ☐ Fresh meats
- ☐ Beer & liquor, if desired in addition to duty free purchases

Entertainment items: for the cabin

- ☐ Digital device to play music and view movies
- ☐ A good book, magazines

Packing items for fishing

- ☐ Tackle Box, including:
- ☐ Fishing license & Outdoors card (in Ziplock bag)
- ☐ Lake map (in Ziplock bag)
- ☐ Compass
- ☐ Lures, hooks, swivels, sinkers, leaders, packaged bait, etc. (for the

species you're after)
- [ ] Spool of fresh line
- [ ] Needle nose pliers/hemostat
- [ ] Fish stringer (of stout rope, not metal clips)
- [ ] Scissors (especially helpful when cleaning fish)
- [ ] Pocket knife
- [ ] Fillet knife
- [ ] Hook sharpener
- [ ] Sunglasses (polarized, w/ retainer strap)
- [ ] Bug spray
- [ ] Suntan lotion
- [ ] Band-aids
- [ ] Long nose fire starter
- [ ] 2-way radios (when using two boats)
- [ ] GPS device (optional)
- [ ] Fishing poles & reels
- [ ] Depth finder w/ charger
- [ ] Life jacket
- [ ] Utility bag – and its contents (holds emergency items and stores outerwear during warmer times)
- [ ] Small first-aid kit
- [ ] 25' length of rope
- [ ] Roll of duct tape
- [ ] An 8' x 10' poly tarp-folded
- [ ] Paper towel sheets in a Ziplock bag
- [ ] Scrap towel
- [ ] Flashlight

We hang this checklist in the cabin (used in the mornings to assure the boat has what's needed)

☐ Life jackets

☐ Fish filets in Ziplock on ice – if cleaned the evening before

☐ Zip-lock bag with flour

☐ Cooking oil

☐ Salt & pepper

☐ Sandwich lunches & snacks – when not having fried walleye

☐ Beverage cooler, w/ ice, water, drinks

☐ Thermos w/ coffee

☐ Utility bag - for apparel

☐ Tackle boxes w/ lake map, compass (& GPS device)

☐ Depth finder

☐ Rods – reels

☐ Sunglasses

For shore lunch days: in addition to the camp's shore lunch box...

(Ensure their box has a cooking pot, plates, utensils, tongs, serving spoon, and paper towels.)

The following items can be packed in the camp's shore lunch box.

Your own...

☐ Non-stick fry pan

☐ Spatula

☐ Cooking oil

☐ Salt & pepper

☐ Vegetables – ? can opener

The Canadian Fishing Adventure

☐ Firelighter

☐ Oven mitts

☐ Bug spray

Selecting a camp

We repeat here for convenience – the questions we ask camp representatives when considering a location:

Lodging:

    ☐ Describe the bathrooms.

    ☐ Does the cabin have running hot & cold water? Ice?

    ☐ What is the cabin's heat source?

    ☐ Is electricity available? Internet? Phone?

    ☐ Number of people per sleeping room?

    ☐ Is bedding provided? Towels?

Meals:

    ☐ Explain dining options.

    ☐ In the morning, how is coffee made available?

    ☐ Is cooking allowed in the cabin?

    ☐ Can the camp prepare a 'shore lunch' box? Provide an LP burner?

    ☐ Does the lodge sell groceries? Beer/Liquor/Fishing gear?

Fishing:

    ☐ What size and type of fish are being caught daily?

    ☐ Have them describe their boats, motors, and baits available.

    ☐ Do they provide dip nets, minnow buckets, and boat seats w/ backs?

- ☐ Do they have 'fishing guide' services?
- ☐ What are the lake's fish 'in possession' limits?
- ☐ Is there a fish cleaning shack? A fish freezer?

Miscellaneous

- ☐ How do they prefer to be paid? (Cashier's check? Credit card? Cash?)
- ☐ Do they sell fishing licenses?
- ☐ Nearest medical service (Describe what to expect if a health emergency arises.)

www.ingramcontent.com/pod-product-compliance
Lightning Source LLC
LaVergne TN
LVHW021117080426
835512LV00011B/2550